IMAGES
of Aviation

DENVER AIRPORTS
FROM STAPLETON TO DIA

On the Cover: Denver Union Airport was one of the private airports in Denver in the 1920s, before the development of Denver Municipal Airport. Located near Park Hill, Denver Union is representative of the many private airports that were being constructed at the time, which prompted the City of Denver to begin building its own public-use airport. (Courtesy of the Harry M. Rhoades Collection at the Denver Public Library.)

IMAGES
of Aviation

Denver Airports
From Stapleton to DIA

Jeffrey C. Price, Jeffrey S. Forrest,
and Shahn G. Sederberg
Foreword by Ginger Sunday Evans

ARCADIA
PUBLISHING

ISBN 978-1-4671-0240-7

Published by Arcadia Publishing
Charleston, South Carolina

Printed in the United States of America

Library of Congress Control Number: 2018940576

For all general information, please contact Arcadia Publishing:
Telephone 843-853-2070
Fax 843-853-0044
E-mail sales@arcadiapublishing.com
For customer service and orders:
Toll-Free 1-888-313-2665

Visit us on the Internet at www.arcadiapublishing.com

We would like to dedicate this book to all the people who have helped make the Denver airport a success.

Contents

Foreword

Denver's Marvelous Field of Dreams

It was clear that a new international airport for Colorado was needed. Stapleton and its 1920s-era site had runways too closely spaced to accommodate Denver's occasional stormy conditions. The best site for a new airport was also clear—an affordable, large (no, *huge*) greenfield site was available just outside the planned I-470 beltway. The site was farther from the Rocky Mountains than Stapleton and adjacent to a massive power transmission line. Nearly a hundred runway and terminal configurations were modeled to design the most efficient airport layout in the world, on a 53-square-mile site that allowed adequate space for five decades of growth. Another six-square-mile corridor allowed continuous high-speed interstate access and space for connecting utilities, rail, and future development. By overlapping the master plan, environmental process, and design, and driven by the innovative and hardworking people of Colorado, the massively complex infrastructure project was completed in a yet-to-be matched record time. From start of the master plan in May 1985 to opening day in February 1994, it covered just eight years and ten months.

DIA, now known as DEN, or Denver International Airport, is a leader in sustainability, starting with design standards that required use of energy efficient glazing and equipment, the first onsite recycling plant for aircraft deicing fluids, and support for shared transportation services. Integrated art and respectful archeological studies are part of DIA's heritage—just one example of Denver's commitment to diversity. DIA provides award-winning customer service and evolving and joyful amenities. It was the first US airport to have fully NextGen air traffic capability and continues to support three hub airline operations. That passenger traffic has grown from 34 million in its first year to 60 million–plus in 2017 is a testament to the peerless efficiency of its runway and linear concourse configuration.

One can take a back road to the south entrance of DIA and view fields of sunflowers and wheat that once continued across the airport's expanse. The terminal complex rises up from that view, like a white Oz but a very real airport city of dreams come true.

—Ginger Sunday Evans, MS, PE
Former Chief of New Airport Construction
Former Director of Aviation

ACKNOWLEDGMENTS

We would like to thank the following for their help in compiling this book: Kim Day (CEO), Stacey Stegman (vice president of communications, marketing, and customer service), Tracey Wright (special events manager), Jeannette Hilaire (manager of airport planning), and all of Denver International Airport. Thanks also go to Zig and Dianne Price, Barb Swarts, Haitham Kassab, Dave Ulane, Abhaya Tripathi, Sanjay Tripathi, Dennis Heap, and of course, our families, who continue to support our writing endeavors.

Unless otherwise noted, all photographs in this work come from Denver International Airport (DEN), the Hart collection at the Colorado Historical Society (CHS), the Otto Perry collection at the Denver Public Library (OR-DPL), the Western History and Genealogy Department of the Denver Public Library (WH-DPL), or the Harry M. Rhoades collection of the Denver Public Library (HR-DPL).

INTRODUCTION

The city council said it would cost too much. The business community said it was too far away from the city. The citizens did not want their tax dollars used to build it. The newspapers rejected it as the mayor's folly. Pilots, including the great Charles Lindberg, opposed the location of it, and everyone complained that the site was selected through political favoritism. Ironically, the arguments used to oppose the original Denver Municipal Airport in 1929 were nearly the same as those used to oppose Denver International Airport 66 years later.

This is the story of three airports and how they brought the city from cow town to boom town. During the early days of the western frontier, the original pioneers and the wagon trains had difficulty crossing the Continental Divide. When the transcontinental railroad went north through Cheyenne, the fledgling city of Denver and its surrounding towns and counties were left behind. The city responded by connecting a rail line from Cheyenne to Denver, but then saw a second chance to be the critical link in the coast-to-coast connection by capitalizing on the newest technology, the airplane. However, when the airmail routes also went north through Cheyenne, city visionaries realized that unless they did something bold, their cow town could soon become a ghost town.

On the cusp of the Great Depression, Denver mayor Benjamin Stapleton pushed for the development of the first city-operated airport. Denver Municipal Airport opened in 1929 with three hub airlines: United, Continental, and Frontier. While Stapleton was honored to have the airport named after him, by the mid-1980s, the name had become synonymous with congestion, flight delays, and frequent closures when snow moved in. To solve the problem, Denver mayor Federico Peña envisioned a massive new airport, but when Denver International Airport (DIA) opened in 1995, its three hub airlines had whittled away to just one, and critics warned of dire consequences. Yet the airport persevered, and today, with its iconic tent roof, six runways, and 53 square miles of land, it stands as one of the most beautiful and busiest airports in the world.

The development of Denver's airport is as much representative of the change in how we look at the world and our development as citizens of the United States as how our airports have changed. Denver's first airport was the vision of a man, Benjamin Stapleton, who was heavily associated with the Ku Klux Klan. A little over 50 years later, Denver's first Hispanic mayor, Federico Peña, envisioned Denver's newest airport and got the city started on a bold new path. What Peña started, Denver's first African American mayor, Wellington Webb, finished when he officially opened DIA on February 28, 1995.

The DIA of today is very different than it was nearly 30 years ago when it first opened. Through mergers and buyouts, a small handful of airlines now dominate the industry, but times will change again. The industry sits on the precipice of the evolution of unmanned aerial vehicles and, soon, spaceport development. However, DIA, now officially called DEN, is not only a beautiful creation but also has the ability and leadership to continue to benefit Denver, its surrounding cities and counties, and the state of Colorado for years to come.

The authors wish to share that the focus of this book is not a list of simple facts about the airport, although those are noted where appropriate. We instead tried to discover the underlying stories behind what the public sees, and the connecting and recurrent themes in building both airports. We had far more research and found more stories than we had room for in this book. The history of the airlines in Denver is as rich and intriguing as the history of the airport, but there are only so many pages to fill. Also, there were many photographs, many of them iconic, that we were unable to secure the rights for.

One

Aviation Comes to Colorado

The Origin of the Denver Airport

Benjamin Stapleton, mayor of Denver (1923–1931 and 1935–1947) and Charles Vail, a famous highway engineer, envisioned an airport that would establish Denver at the forefront of the fledgling aviation industry. Their vision established Denver Municipal Airport, which would later evolve into the fifth busiest airport in the United States and the 18th busiest in the world. Initial construction of Denver Municipal Airport was completed by the summer of 1929 and included just an administration building and a hangar with a lean-to maintenance shop. A smaller building housed the airport's fire-fighting equipment, ambulance, and a central heating plant. The airport opened despite strong opposition from city councilmen who contended that its land was bought to pay back political favors. Citizen complaints about tax dollars being used for aviation and businessmen complaining that it was too far away from the city also caused problems for the airport. Despite these problems, Denver Municipal Airport was established initially with three airlines committed to starting air service. (Courtesy of DPL.)

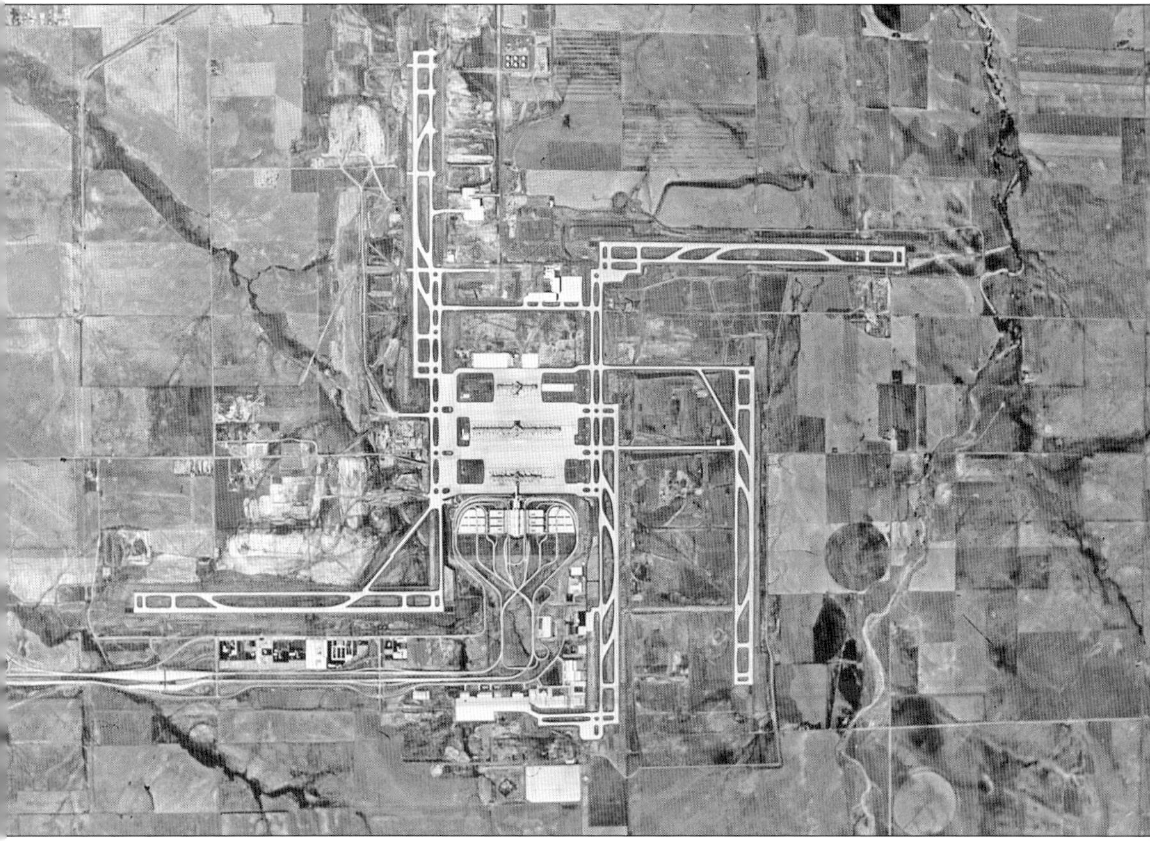

Located in east Denver, the original Denver Municipal Airport would undergo a name change to Stapleton Airport, then eventually a move 23 miles northeast of downtown Denver to become Denver International Airport. In an epic evening known as "Push Night," airport operators closed one international airport and opened another within hours of each other. Today, Denver International Airport features six runways and over 100 airline gates, and occupies 53 square miles of land, making it larger than the island of Manhattan in New York City. (Courtesy of DPL.)

The Rocky Mountains were an obstacle for travel to and from early Denver. This photograph taken between 1885 and 1890 shows that only the most stalwart pioneers, using mule teams and wagons, dared to travel through Ute Pass in El Paso County, Colorado. The Rockies proved too much of a challenge for both the railroads and the air mail service, which both headed north to Cheyenne to bypass Denver's higher mountain ranges. (Courtesy of WH-DPL.)

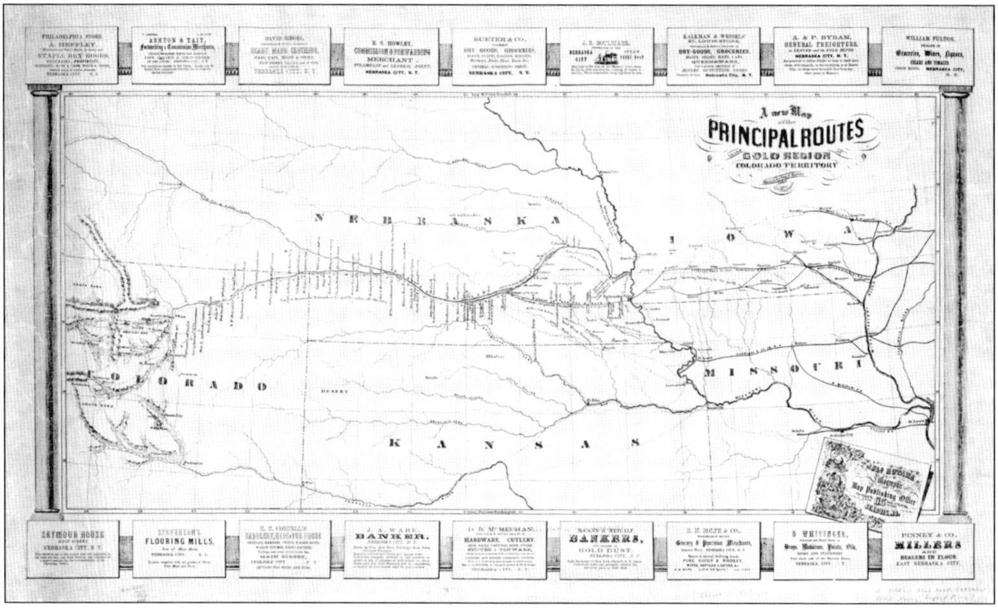

Railroads, rivers, and territorial boundaries can be seen in this c. 1862 gold rush map promoting Nebraska City as a supply center. Despite its position near the middle of the United States, Denver has long struggled to establish and maintain itself as an essential waypoint for travelers heading west, due to the challenge of crossing the Rocky Mountains. (Courtesy of WH-DPL.)

The opening of the American frontier made the West a popular tourist attraction. Reflective of today's airliners, Trains hauled luggage and cargo and had certain cars dedicated to business clientele and leisure passengers. Seen here, 19th-century leisure passengers take a break on an excursion trip up Clear Creek Canyon in Jefferson County, Colorado. (Courtesy of the Dr. Nolie Mumey collection and DPL.)

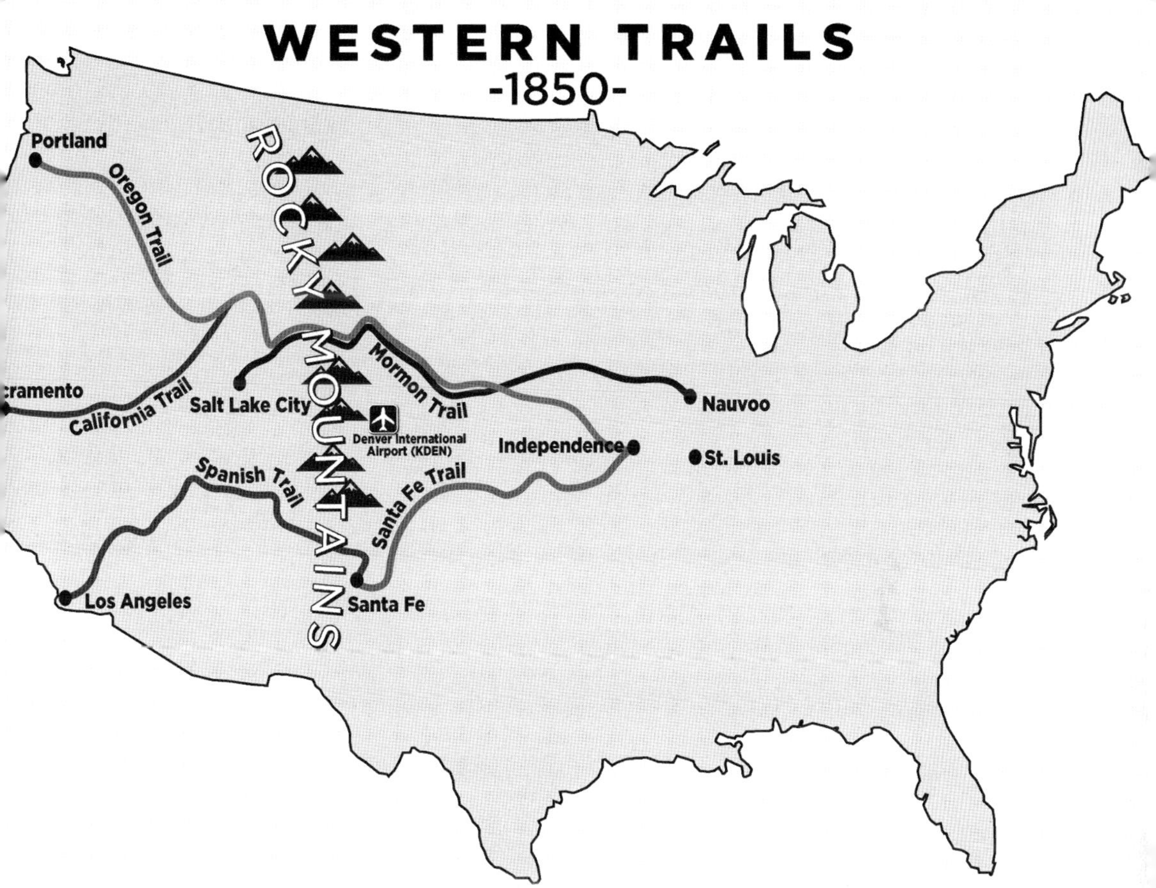

In the early days of expansion across the country, the wagon trains found it just as difficult as the railroads and the early air mail industry to cross the Colorado Rockies. The major trails went north to Wyoming or south to New Mexico, where the mountains were easier to cross. (Courtesy of Shahn Sederberg.)

This is believed to be the first known image of an airplane flying in the Denver area, an early biplane flying over a flat landscape. Even the invention of the airplane did not immediately solve Denver's proximity to the Rockies issue. Many pilots felt that aircraft could not climb high enough to fly over the mountains, coupled with the fact that Denver itself sits at an elevation of 5,280 feet. Many early aircraft had difficulty taking off at higher elevations. (Courtesy of HR-DPL.)

In 1909, *The Denver Post* offered $10,000 for the first successful demonstration of mechanically propelled flight in Colorado. On February 1, 1910, just over a month after the deadline, Louis Paulhan, the French "birdman" took off from Overland Park in southwest Denver. Between 40,000 and 50,000 people were in attendance. Paulhan unfortunately crashed the plane two days later, injuring three people and seeing much of his plane stolen by souvenir seekers. (Courtesy of HR-DPL.)

Private investors opened Curtiss Aviation Field, one of the first aerodromes in Denver. Situated on Colorado Boulevard in the northeast section of Denver, it was later renamed Park Hill Airport, and then Hayden Airport. Many of the nation's original airports were operated by private enterprise out of necessity. The growing desire to use aircraft required building airports. (Courtesy of DPL.)

In 1925, Carrie Bella became Denver's first parachutist. Parachute designs of the time were similar to what would later be used in World War II, most famously during the assault by the 82nd and 101st Airborne Divisions during the invasion of Normandy. (Both, courtesy of HR-DPL.)

Noted physician Dr. Nolie Mumey is pictured in front of a water-cooled airplane. Many of the photographs in this book are attributed to him. Mumey was a member of the US Army Medical Corps in France during World War I and flew in the Colorado National Guard. He passed away in 1984. (Courtesy of DPL.)

Denver's second transportation crisis came when the transcontinental airmail routes were mapped and Cheyenne was again selected over Denver as the central western mail stop. The passage of the Kelly Air Mail Act in 1925 opened up bids for private airplane operators to pick up feeder mail routes to the transcontinental route. Colorado Airways won the Cheyenne-Denver-Pueblo contract and started flying it in 1926. (Courtesy of DPL.)

Consolidating Denver's aviation community was seen as the only way to get to the forefront of the growing industry. Mayor Benjamin Stapleton and his commissioner of parks and improvements, Charles Vail, felt a municipal airport owned and operated by the City of Denver that offered modern equipment and services would draw both airlines and pilots. (Courtesy of WH-DPL.)

Several sites were suggested for the new airport, but Stapleton and Vail favored the Sand Creek site, about six miles from the center of downtown. However, H. Brown Cannon, a personal friend of the mayor, owned a large portion of the site and an option for more parcels that would be needed. Cannon stood to profit substantially if the city bought both parcels; however, no illegality on Cannon or Stapleton's part was ever proven. Sixty years later, similar allegations of political cronyism resurfaced during the acquisition of land for Denver International Airport. (Courtesy of DEN.)

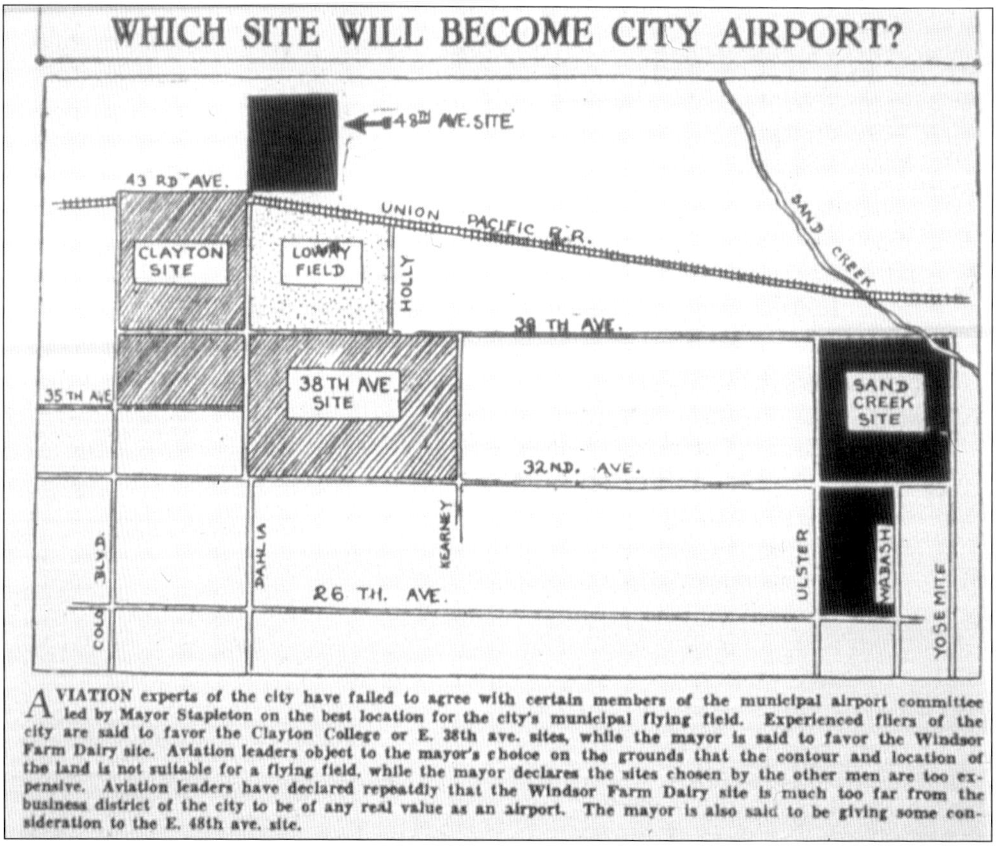

WHICH SITE WILL BECOME CITY AIRPORT?

AVIATION experts of the city have failed to agree with certain members of the municipal airport committee led by Mayor Stapleton on the best location for the city's municipal flying field. Experienced fliers of the city are said to favor the Clayton College or E. 38th ave. sites, while the mayor is said to favor the Windsor Farm Dairy site. Aviation leaders object to the mayor's choice on the grounds that the contour and location of the land is not suitable for a flying field, while the mayor declares the sites chosen by the other men are too expensive. Aviation leaders have declared repeatdly that the Windsor Farm Dairy site is much too far from the business district of the city to be of any real value as an airport. The mayor is also said to be giving some consideration to the E. 48th ave. site.

Famed aviator Charles A. Lindbergh stopped in Denver in 1927 as part of his national tour to promote aviation. In this photograph, he stands by a Ryan B-1 Brougham, manufactured by Ryan Aeronautical, which also built the *Spirit of St. Louis*. When asked about the location of the new airport, Lindberg said colocating with the existing Lowry military base was the better plan over the Sand Creek site. (Courtesy of HR-DPL.)

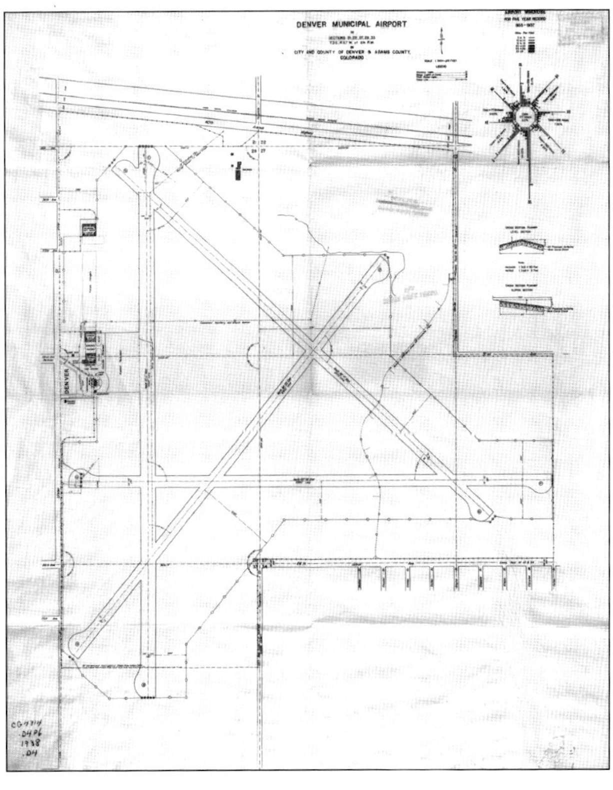

This 1938 schematic of Denver Municipal Airport shows the existing and planned future runways. In order to receive the Department of Commerce's A-1 rating, Denver's high-elevation runways needed to be at least 3,300 feet long. When finally constructed, the north-south runway was 4,050 feet and the east-west runway 4,650 feet. (Courtesy of WH-DPL.)

During construction of Denver Municipal Airport, Lita Grey Chaplin, an American actress and the second wife of Charlie Chaplin, prepares to take a flight at the privately owned Denver Union Airport. The Sunbeam Air Transport Company specialized in providing scenic rides to the public, most of whom had never seen their towns and homes from the air. (Courtesy of WH-DPL.)

The Public Service Company of Colorado installed an elaborate lighting system at the new airport. This high-intensity light cast a beam in a 180-degree arc just six feet off the ground. When the beam hit an inbound plane, the pilot knew the aircraft was six feet up. (Courtesy of HR-DPL.)

By 1927, the *Rocky Mountain News* reported that pilots on the site selection committee were almost unanimous in their opposition to the Sand Creek site. Other opponents were concerned about the sandy soil, which was thought to be too porous to support runways, while others thought the airport was too far from downtown Denver. Proponents of another site, Lowry Airfield, the home of the 120th National Guard Squadron, which was financed by the state of Colorado and was closer to downtown, argued that expenses could be shared with the National Guard. One city councilman expressed that he not only opposed the site, but the concept of the city spending taxpayer money to finance and operate a municipal airport. This is a national debate that continues to this day. Even *The Denver Post* called the airport "Stapleton's Folly," but in the end, the mayor would not be denied his new airport. (Courtesy of DEN.)

Seen here is the "Eye of Denver," a high-intensity beacon mounted on top of the airport administration building that pilots could see from miles away. The first floor of the three-story building was designated for passenger use. The second floor housed the airport administration offices, three suites to lease to private operators, and pilot amenities including a pilot sleep room, showers, and a radio room. The third floor was the meteorological section. (Courtesy of WH-DPL.)

The airport hangar was painted bright orange so it could be seen more easily by approaching pilots, and for its time was one of the larger hangars constructed. It could accommodate 12 of the largest transport aircraft at the time. (Courtesy of WH-DPL.)

Pictured here is the two-story residence for the airport manager. In the early days of aviation, it was not uncommon for a city to hire an airport manager and provide housing on or near the airport. (Courtesy of WH-DPL.)

Water commissioner Findley McFarland, head of McFarland Auto Company, is seen here with a baby deer, the airport's mascot. Ironically, today's airport managers are highly concerned with wildlife on and around the runways and the hazards they pose to flight operations. (Courtesy of CHS.)

By the fall of 1929, the Denver Municipal Airport had cost the City of Denver approximately $430,000 from land acquisition to construction. The dedication program called it the "Union Station of the Air," and announced, "Denver citizens have the knowledge that their city boasts one of the finest airports in the land. That this achievement in building places it in the forefront of progressive cities which are meeting the problems arising from the rapid development of a new method of commercial transportation and that its fame will be advanced wherever planes land or take off, which means nearly every spot on the face of the globe." (Courtesy of WH-DPL.)

On Thursday, October 17, 1929, Denver Municipal Airport officially opened. Four days of celebrations included pylon racing and other aerial contests, military formation flying and aerobatics demonstrations, and live ordnance drops onto a silhouette village erected on the southeast side of the north-south runway. (Courtesy of WH-DPL.)

Opening day of the airport extended well into the evening. While there were no official activities planned for the first night, a parade of cars began circling the borders of the airport. Airport staff turned on floodlights and border lights to provide the crowd a little entertainment. Unfortunately, Mayor Stapleton, the driving force for the airport, missed the opening ceremony, as he was hospitalized and recuperating from pneumonia. (Courtesy of WH-DPL.)

On Saturday, October 19, 1929, Army Air Corps pilots performed a series of aerobatic maneuvers for crowds at the airport, doing barrel rolls, loops, slow rolls, and inverted flight. By that afternoon, the Army planes took to the skies for a formation review over the new airport. (Courtesy of WH-DPL.)

At the Denver Municipal Airport, reporters interview Adm. Richard E. Byrd after his historic flight to the South Pole in the Fokker trimotor, named the *Floyd Bennett*, shown here. Byrd and his crew of three passed over the South Pole on November 29, 1929. (Courtesy of HR-DPL.)

Spectators view biplanes of the Colorado Air National Guard at Denver Municipal Airport. (Courtesy of HR-DPL.)

By Sunday, October 20, 1929, an estimated 50,000 people arrived to see the new airport. Free flying trips were given to over 1,000 people, and Gov. William Adams proclaimed October 14–19 Airmail Week. Airport manager William Wunderlick and his assistants gave guided tours of the airport, and more than 60 planes were on hand for inspection by the public. Despite objections from city councilmen, pilots, and planners, Denver had its airport. One week later, on October 29, 1929, the stock market crashed, sending the United States into the Great Depression. (Courtesy of DPL.)

Amelia Earhart is standing next to Frederick G. Bonfils at Denver's airport near a Beech Nut Autogyro in 1931. Earhart said she would fly in a series of tests for the Beech-Nut packing company. Earhart's importance in advancing the cause of women in aviation continues to have a positive impact to this day. (Courtesy of HR-DPL.)

In 1927, Western Air Express took over the original Cheyenne-Denver-Pueblo airmail route from Colorado Airways, and eventually became Western Airlines. This c. 1934 photograph shows passengers embarking on a Western Airlines aircraft in front of Denver's terminal. Many of the original mail companies became the nation's first airlines. A month before the airport opened, three airlines announced they were preparing to start operations from the Denver base: Western Air Express with its Cheyenne-Denver-Pueblo airmail feeder route, US Airways Inc. with its Denver–Kansas City airmail route, and Mid-Continent Express with its Denver–El Paso route. (Courtesy of HR-DPL.)

This 1934 photograph shows several pilots standing in front of a Western Airlines Boeing 247. The B-247 entered service in 1933 and was the first twin-engine aircraft capable of flying on one engine, which represented a significant increase in air safety. (Donated by Harry Davidson, courtesy of CHS.)

The first privately owned airplane to fly into Denver Municipal Airport, NC605N, is seen here in May 1930 with Sam Moser (left) and Fr. Edward S. Muenich. Warren Prosser owned the aircraft. (Courtesy of DPL.)

In an early recognition of the value of aircraft to business, this biplane features the lettering "Phillips Petroleum Co. Bartlesville, Okla." The fuel truck adjacent to the plane is also from the Phillips Petroleum Company. (Courtesy of WH-DPL.)

This experimental aircraft was manufactured at the Gray Goose Airways facility on Josephine Street in 1931. The Denver metropolitan area has a rich history in aerospace manufacturing, and Colorado consistently ranks amongst the highest in aerospace employment in the United States, along with California, Texas, and Florida. This photograph was taken by Otto C. Perry. (Courtesy of DPL.)

One of the largest commercial planes of its time, the Ford Tri-Motor, is seen here at Denver Municipal Airport around 1930. The Tri-Motor was the first aircraft to fly over the South Pole, and Pres. Franklin D. Roosevelt used one in his 1932 election campaign. The aircraft, popular with passengers and airline operators, played a major role in convincing the public that air travel was safe. (Courtesy of CHS.)

Here is an American Gyron Crusader experimental aircraft designed by Tommy Shelton, with Ray Wilson as the test pilot. The plane was built and flown in Denver in 1935 and was one of two experimental aircraft flown at Denver Municipal Airport. (Courtesy of CHS.)

In 1936, the summer air show featured the National Balloon Races and the Mile High Air Races. Mayor Benjamin Stapleton took his first airplane flight during the three-day air show. The 20-minute flight gave the mayor his first aerial view of the city. (Courtesy of WH-DPL.)

Curtis P-1s and A-3s are seen at Denver Municipal Airport. The P-1s were the first aircraft serving both the Army Air Corps and the US Navy. (Courtesy of CHS.)

While United Air Lines had been serving Denver's airport under a lease agreement with Wyoming Air Service since 1935, United did not officially began service until 1937, with the first regularly scheduled flight between Denver and Cheyenne. United also applied to have Denver designated as a regular airmail stop rather than a spur off the main route. (Courtesy of DPL.)

This photograph shows a Texaco truck with "Continental Air Lines" painted on the side and parked in front of Hangar No. 2 at the Denver Municipal Airport. Continental started service in Denver in 1937, connecting Denver to El Paso, and soon moved its headquarters to Denver Municipal Airport. (Courtesy of WH-DPL.)

This photograph shows an airplane flying over the growing city of Denver. In 1940, Congress created the Civil Aeronautics Board, which took over control of approving airline routes, airfares, and schedules. Combined with funding through President Roosevelt's Works Progress Administration, Denver was set to become an important part of the nation's aviation plans. (Courtesy of CHS.)

By 1938, federal money allowed Denver Municipal Airport to extend, strengthen, and pave several of its runways and acquire more parcels of land, opening the airport for more expansion. The airport also got its first control tower that year. The tower, called the "Matchbox," sat atop the administration building with an "air cop" in charge. The air cops used two-way radios or a portable red-green light gun that could be seen for up to 10 miles during the day and 20 miles at night to communicate with pilots. (Courtesy of CHS.)

On August 25, 1944, Denver Municipal Airport was renamed Stapleton Airfield in honor of Mayor Benjamin Stapleton, who not only envisioned the new airport but used it to help Denver grow as a city. A dinner put together by Continental, United, and Western Airlines was held in his honor at the Brown Palace Hotel in downtown Denver. The airport generated much-needed jobs during the difficult Depression and war years. More revenue was created through the federal funds used to expand the airport. By 1945, the airport averaged 40 to 50 flights a day, employed over 1,200 people, and had two flying schools and four major airlines. (Courtesy of DEN.)

In 1948, actor Scott Brady, in town for the premier of his movie *Canon City*, is seen here handcuffed to state prison warden Roy Best at Stapleton Airfield. (Courtesy of WH-DPL.)

A United Air Lines DC-4 is parked in front of the Denver Stapleton Airfield terminal. The United Aircraft & Transport Company included several aircraft and engine manufacturers such as Boeing, Pratt & Whitney, Sikorsky, Stearman, and Northrop Airlines. The conglomerate broke apart during the upheaval of the airmail industry in early 1934, but reformed months later with Boeing and Stearman departing as a result of legislation that prohibited aircraft manufacturers from also providing air transportation. The new holding company was called United Air Lines and officially started service in Denver in 1937. (Courtesy of CHS.)

This is the interior of the United Air Lines office at Stapleton Airfield. As an early adopter of Stapleton as a base of operations, United would continue to help the airport grow, even when the federal government would not. When Denver's airport was given low priority by the government for radio beacons, which would allow aircraft to operate safely at night, United installed two beacons along the Nebraska-Colorado route, with the promise the government would pay them back later, which it did. (Courtesy of DPL.)

The early passenger routes followed the already established airmail routes. The coast-to-coast route was US Mail Route 1, which quickly became known as the Main Line. In the late 1930s, United Air Lines had adopted "the Main Line Airway" theme along with a new slogan, "More than a route, a standard of service," to convey the importance the airline placed on safety and passenger comfort. This photograph shows a United Air Lines DC-3 carrying the moniker "Mainliner." (Courtesy of DEN.)

This photograph shows a DC-6 parked in front of the Stapleton terminal on May 5, 1958. Continental Air Lines started service at Denver's airport in 1937, the same year as United. The two airlines had even more in common, as Continental was previously operated under the United umbrella as Varney Air Lines. As Varney's financial position grew more precarious, the company agreed to sell Robert F. Six a 40-percent share in the company. United's president, W.A. "Pat" Patterson, even loaned Six several two-way radios for his new fleet. (Courtesy of WH-DPL.)

Continental Airlines is largely the story of one man, Robert F. Six. A former lieutenant colonel in the Army Air Corps Transport Command during World War II, he eventually won a series of routes from the Civil Aeronautics Board and established agreements with other airlines to continue to expand service throughout the country. This photograph shows Continental mechanics with a DC-3 parked in front of their hangar at the south end of Stapleton. (Courtesy of CHS.)

Frontier Airlines formed in 1950 through the merger of Monarch Airlines (which was already operating at Stapleton), Challenger Airlines, and Arizona Airways. The airline began operation at Stapleton Airfield that same year. Frontier slowly gained recognition in an already crowded field, but by this time, the airline had a network in place through the Rocky Mountain region. Frontier expanded its route miles, which expanded its revenue base. (Courtesy of DEN.)

Radar was installed at Stapleton in the early 1950s. Radar sends radio waves that reflect back to an antenna and can determine the location and velocity of an object. It was secretly developed before World War II as an early warning system for detecting incoming enemy aircraft. Radar's use expanded after the war to help air-traffic controllers maintain aircraft separation and guide pilots during bad weather. (Courtesy of CHS.)

Two

Stapleton International Airport

The Golden Age of Flight

In early 1953, with an average of 750–800 planes a day flying into and out of Stapleton, the Civil Aeronautics Agency constructed a new six-story control tower (lower left). A year later, the old terminal building was razed and replaced with an expanded facility. Also, in recognition of the importance of the airlines' revenue, the city used both bonds and federal grant money to construct hangars for both United and Continental Airlines. (Courtesy of CHS.)

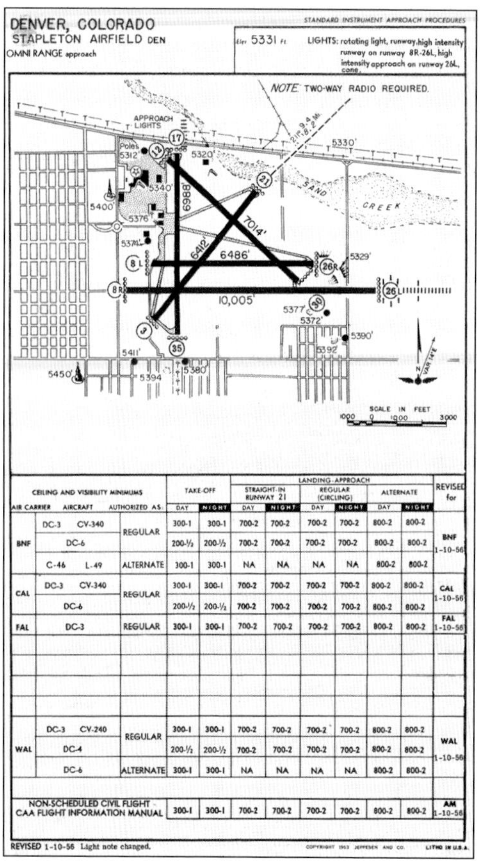
DENVER, COLORADO
STAPLETON AIRFIELD DEN
OMNI RANGE approach

STANDARD INSTRUMENT APPROACH PROCEDURES

Elev 5331 Ft LIGHTS: rotating light, runway high intensity runway on runway 8R-26L, high intensity approach on runway 26L, cone.

CEILING AND VISIBILITY MINIMUMS			TAKE-OFF		LANDING-APPROACH STRAIGHT-IN RUNWAY 21		REGULAR (CIRCLING)		ALTERNATE		REVISED for
AIR CARRIER	AIRCRAFT	AUTHORIZED AS:	DAY	NIGHT	DAY	NIGHT	DAY	NIGHT	DAY	NIGHT	
BNF	DC-3 CV-340	REGULAR	300-1	300-1	700-2	700-2	700-2	700-2	800-2	800-2	BNF 1-10-56
	DC-6		200-½	200-½	700-2	700-2	700-2	700-2	800-2	800-2	
	C-46 L-49	ALTERNATE	300-1	300-1	NA	NA	NA	NA	800-2	800-2	
CAL	DC-3 CV-340	REGULAR	300-1	300-1	700-2	700-2	700-2	700-2	800-2	800-2	CAL 1-10-56
	DC-6		200-½	200-½	700-2	700-2	700-2	700-2	800-2	800-2	
FAL	DC-3	REGULAR	300-1	300-1	700-2	700-2	700-2	700-2	800-2	800-2	FAL 1-10-56
WAL	DC-3 CV-240	REGULAR	300-1	300-1	700-2	700-2	700-2	700-2	800-2	800-2	WAL 1-10-56
	DC-4		200-½	200-½	700-2	700-2	700-2	700-2	800-2	800-2	
	DC-6	ALTERNATE	300-1	300-1	NA	NA	NA	NA	800-2	800-2	
NON-SCHEDULED CIVIL FLIGHT - CAA FLIGHT INFORMATION MANUAL			300-1	300-1	700-2	700-2	700-2	700-2	800-2	800-2	AM 1-10-56

REVISED 1-10-56 Light note changed. COPYRIGHT 1953 JEPPESEN AND CO. LITHO IN U.S.A.

In January 1955, the terminal expansion was completed and included a new north wing. For the first time, passengers could retrieve their bags from indoor carousels and board their flights from covered walkways, while the airlines received more gates and additional ticket counters. Stapleton was ranked the 22nd largest airport in the world. (Courtesy of CHS.)

This 1953 airport directory chart shows the runway and taxiway configuration at Stapleton. (Courtesy of FAA.)

During the 1950s, national statistics showed that more individuals could fly on private planes (referred to as general aviation, or GA) than on commercial planes. But this boom came at a cost as commercial airports became more congested, often forcing many GA operators to smaller airports. GA accounted for 50 percent of Stapleton's flight operations and represented the airport's fastest growing market. In 1956, the city leased Combs Aviation 315,000 square feet to build 50 more hangars northwest of the terminal to be used by private aircraft. (Courtesy of DEN.)

On November 1, 1955, United Air Lines Denver Mainliner Flight 629 exploded into a fireball just 11 minutes after taking off from Stapleton, killing all 44 on board. Jack Gilbert Graham was convicted of bombing the flight by putting dynamite into his mother's suitcase, unbeknownst to her. He then took out $37,500 worth of flight insurance on her. Graham was found guilty of the crime and died in 1957 in Colorado's gas chamber. This was the first confirmed airline bombing in the United States where an individual was caught and convicted of the crime. (Courtesy of the Federal Bureau of Investigation.)

Stapleton was growing rapidly, so in 1956, Denver mayor J. Quigg Newton proposed the creation of an airport authority, which would allow appointed representatives from the airlines, general aviation, and members of the community to have control over the operation of the airport. However, the change would take airport revenue away from the city and redirect it all to the airport. The proposition never moved forward. Today, FAA restrictions prevent airport revenues from being used for anything other than the direct benefit of the airport, regardless of the airport ownership structure. (Courtesy of CHS.)

In 1956, several studies were conducted to determine how to prepare the airport for the faster and heavier jet planes being used by airlines. The existing north-south runway, the two parallel east-west runways, and two diagonal runways were inadequate for use by jet aircraft. Denver mayor Will Nicholson told the *Rocky Mountain News* that he was not sure if Stapleton could handle jet airliners. This photograph shows runway construction to accommodate the new jet aircraft at Stapleton. (Courtesy of DEN.)

Air cargo has always been an important revenue source for Denver's airports. A Flying Tiger Line Lockheed Super H Constellation, as pictured here, established the first nonstop, transcontinental airfreight schedule. The aircraft was capable of carrying 43,000 pounds of freight at 300 miles per hour over a range of 2,500 miles. (Courtesy of WH-DPL.)

On July 11, 1961, a United Airlines Douglas DC-8 arriving from Omaha, Nebraska, crashed while landing at Stapleton, killing 18 people. The aircraft skidded off the east-west runway and burst into flames when the wingtip hit a 30-inch concrete slab on a nearby construction site. However, Stapleton's worst on-airport accident was yet to come. On November 15, 1987, Continental Flight 1713, a DC-9, crashed while taking off on runway 35L, killing 28 of the 82 people on board. (Courtesy of CHS.)

In 1962, just nine years after the construction of the six-story tower, a new fourteen-story air-traffic control tower was constructed. Its elevators were constructed to handle a potential hotel and Sky Chefs catering offices. While the hotel/air-traffic control tower idea never materialized, a 50-seat movie theater showing short travelogue films was built between the new control tower and the adjacent restaurant. By the early 1970s, the theater closed as the airport needed more space. (Courtesy of DEN.)

By the mid-1950s, the nation's air-traffic control system, which was designed for slower propeller driven planes, was straining to handle the faster jet aircraft, leading to a series of accidents. In 1956, a deadly mid-air collision between a United Air Lines DC-7 and a TWA Constellation over the Grand Canyon killed all 128 people on both flights and spurred Congress to focus the industry more on safety and less on commerce. In 1958, the Civil Aeronautics Agency became the Federal Aviation Agency and, by 1966, was renamed the Federal Aviation Administration and moved under the Department of Transportation. (Courtesy of DEN.)

In 1959, Stapleton Airfield entered the jet age with a Continental Boeing 707 becoming the first regularly scheduled jetliner to fly from the airport. TWA's first flight from Europe to Denver occurred in 1960, but Denver did not officially become an international airport until Western Airlines flew nonstop from Calgary to Stapleton in 1968. The 707 can be seen here at far left. (Courtesy of DEN.)

Passengers walk through the newly expanded terminal in 1966. The new terminal was six times the size of the old one and featured a great hall, opening up space for gift shops and more restaurants. The great hall concept would continue in the design of Denver International Airport. (Courtesy of DEN.)

United moved its flight training school from Cheyenne to Denver in 1943. By August 1968, the school moved into a new $30 million facility just west of Stapleton Airfield. United has a long history in the Denver area, even remaining at Stapleton after the airport closed. In 2016, United began consolidating its global pilot training operations to the Stapleton site. This photograph shows the construction of the original flight training facility. (Courtesy of CHS.)

These are some of the early flight simulators at the United Air Lines Flight Training Center, located just west of the newly anointed Stapleton International Airport. By 2018, United's expanded facility, located adjacent to the existing building, housed an additional 30 flight simulators. (Courtesy of CHS.)

By 1964, the Denver Chamber of Commerce wanted to change the airport's name to Denver International Airport, hoping it would lead to more direct international flights. However, the Denver City Council would only agree to Stapleton International Airport. By 1967, concourse C, seen here on the far left, was being completed; a year earlier, the check-in drive had been completed. (Courtesy of DEN.)

This image shows Runway 35L crossing over Interstate 70. This area became a daily logjam during rush hour traffic and continued to do so even after the airport closed. The runway and associated taxiway were eventually torn down after the airport closed. (Courtesy of DEN.)

Construction on concourse D was completed in 1972. The dog leg–shaped concourse included moving walkways down its center. A third level was added to the parking garage, and the baggage claim area was extended. This 1971 photograph shows an early stage of the concourse D construction. A monorail system connecting each concourse was dropped from the final plans. Also at this time, residents of the nearby Park Hill neighborhood began raising concerns about airport noise. (Courtesy of CHS.)

Between July 1969 and June 1972, the United States reported 95 hijackings. By 1972, the FAA required airports to search passengers using metal detectors and search passenger belongings, something many airlines were already doing voluntarily. Police and explosive detection dogs were deployed to the airport, and airfield gates were locked. In 1976, Stapleton experienced its first hijacking when an aircraft that had been hijacked from Grand Island, Nebraska, landed. FBI agents killed the hijacker shortly after landing. (Courtesy of DEN.)

General aviation continued to bring flight operations and revenue to Stapleton throughout the 1970s. This photograph shows the ramp area at Atlas Aviation, a fixed-base operator (FBO). FBOs provide aircraft, pilot, and passenger services to private aircraft operators. FBOs also provide products such as fuel, oil, and pilot supplies, and services such as maintenance hangars and aircraft handling. FBO facilities include flight planning, weather briefing, and crew sleep rooms. Passengers are accommodated with waiting areas, rest rooms, restaurants, and other amenities. (Courtesy of DEN.)

This picture shows Combs Aircraft, another Stapleton FBO. According to the US Centennial of Flight Commission, Harry B. Combs "lived and breathed the Golden and Jet Age of aviation." Combs built and tested his first plane at the age of 16. He and a partner initially formed Mountain States Aviation, which eventually became Combs Aircraft. During World War II, he trained 9,000 military pilots and later was appointed by Pres. John F. Kennedy to help form the air-traffic control system. He was president of Gates Learjet and, in 1996, was enshrined in the National Aviation Hall of Fame. (Courtesy of DEN.)

Denver Ports of Call was a private aircraft operator, used for members of the Ports of Call Travel Club. The club had its own private terminal at Stapleton and operated both domestic and international flights from 1967 to 1992. This photograph shows a Ports of Call Convair 990 parked on the ramp at Stapleton. The company had a failed restart attempt in the late 1990s, choosing to relocate at Rocky Mountain Metropolitan Airport, a general aviation airport just northwest of Denver. The club ended its operations in 1994. (Courtesy of DEN.)

This photograph shows the passenger pickup and drop off area of Stapleton International Airport. As air traffic increased, so did congestion in these areas. (Courtesy of DEN.)

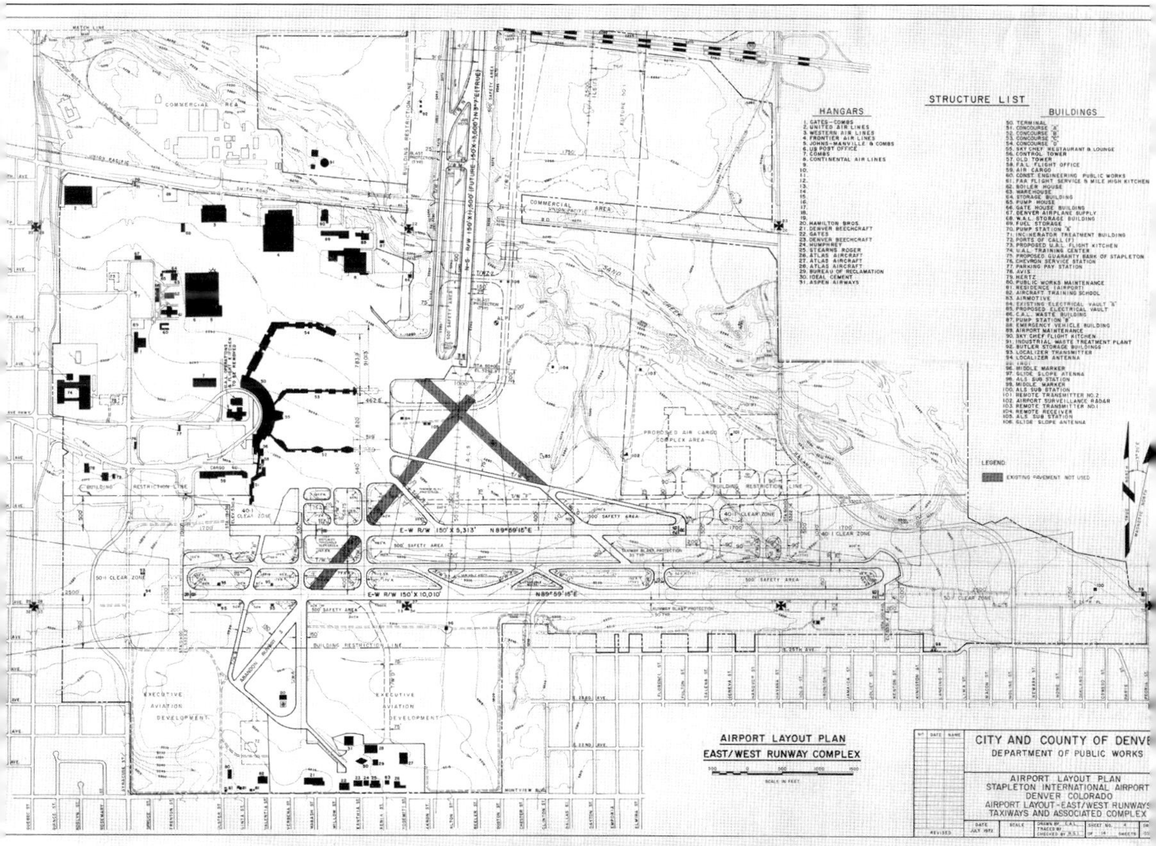

While Stapleton continued to grow, so did airport noise complaints. Although city planners promised Park Hill residents that a new runway would reduce their noise issues, many homeowners had heard this argument before when the airport built the first north-south runway. Studies were commissioned that concluded the airport should either be expanded on its present location, completely moved onto the Rocky Mountain Arsenal land, or relocated. By 1971, the Denver Regional Council of Governments, which represented 30 municipalities and five surrounding counties, including Denver, conducted a federally funded study to determine whether Stapleton should be expanded or relocated to accommodate the growth in air traffic. Although there was talk of relocating the airport, studies by consultants and the airlines suggested the airport could handle the additional traffic by expanding existing runways and building a new north-south runway, located north of Interstate 70. The construction of the new 12,000-foot runway required the acquisition of 622 acres of Rocky Mountain Arsenal land, where the US Army stored nerve gas. This graphic is from the 1972 airport layout plan, showing the proposed new runway, the existing runways, and the decommissioned diagonal runways. (Courtesy of Jeffrey Price and the City and County of Denver, Department of Public Works.)

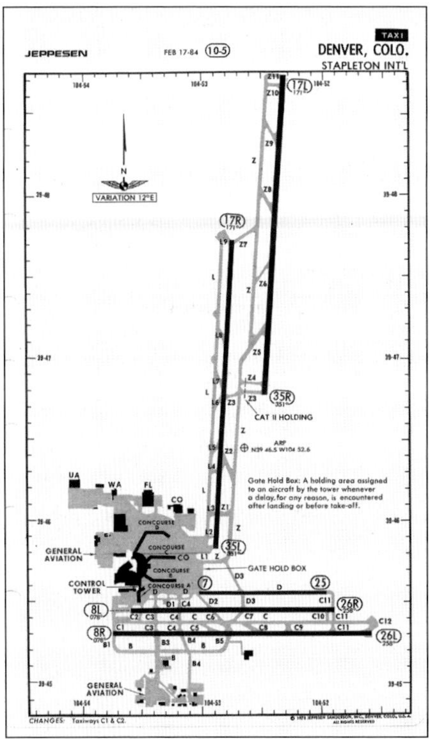

Air-traffic controllers suggested spacing Stapleton's proposed new runway farther away from the existing north-south runway so that simultaneous instrument flight approaches could be used during bad weather. However, the City of Denver said it did not have access to enough land for the necessary spacing. This 1975 photograph shows an expanded terminal complex and grading underway for runway 17L/35R. (Courtesy of DEN.)

This 1975 airport chart shows the location of the new north-south runway, 17L/35R. (Courtesy of FAA.)

Stapleton International Airport received a very special visitor in 1979 when the Space Shuttle *Enterprise* made a stopover en route from Florida to California to conduct flight-testing. The *Enterprise* is shown in this photograph, riding piggyback on top of a B-747. The *Enterprise* was never used in actual space operations and was only constructed for flight test purposes in the atmosphere. (Courtesy of Zig Price.)

In 1979, Frontier Airlines president A.L. Feldman is pictured with Denver mayor William H. "Bill" McNichols at Stapleton International Airport, celebrating the airport's 50th anniversary. Just a year earlier, the US Congress had passed the Deregulation Act allowing the airlines free reign over what cities to serve, which routes to take, and what airfares to charge. Feldman was quoted by the *Rocky Mountain News* as saying, "The public won the benefits of a freer marketplace. Increased competition, or the threat of it, should stimulate the airlines to provide better service and at the lowest possible price." (Courtesy of CHS.)

A row of United Airlines B-727 aircraft is seen here, parked at the gate at Stapleton. Along with Continental Airlines, United had been Stapleton's longest operating airline. However, by 1970, the airline found itself in financial trouble. A new president and CEO was brought in. Eddie Carlson logged 187,000 air miles visiting with United workers, then implemented drastic cuts to schedules, furloughed thousands of employees, cancelled airplane orders, and restructured the company. By 1974, United was showing an $86 million profit. (Courtesy of DEN.)

As passenger traffic grew and new airlines came into the market, delays continued to pile up. By 1989, Stapleton was responsible for 46,000 hours of delay per year, with trickle-down effects that rippled throughout the national air transportation system. Denver's relatively unpredictable weather patterns contributed significantly to the delays, so any solution would have to include an expansion or new airport with multiple runways. (Courtesy of DEN.)

Three

We Said Hello, Goodbye

One Legacy Begins as Another Ends

The 1980s would bring significant changes to Stapleton International Airport, as the full effects of deregulation started to impact the industry. Since the early days of aviation, the federal government had largely controlled commercial air transportation, with the ability to regulate airline fares and determine the routes individual carriers served. The Airline Deregulation Act of 1978 ended the government's economic control of the industry, and things would never be the same again. Deregulation brought a surge in airline bankruptcies, mergers, and acquisitions, with more than 100 airlines either folding or being absorbed between 1983 and 1988. The most significant change, however, came as the airlines adopted the hub-and-spoke network of route distribution. Many smaller airports lost air carrier service, while the airline-hub airports were able to exert more control over the market, with airfares jumping as high as 20 percent. For Stapleton, this meant a huge growth in passenger traffic. By 1989, Stapleton would have a new concourse and a new runway, lose one of its hubbing airlines, Frontier, and see another, Continental, significantly reorganize, and start breaking ground on a brand new airport. (Courtesy of Zig Price.)

While Denver's weather is generally milder than the mountains to the west and the plains to the east, its location causes unpredictable conditions. On Christmas Eve 1982, the snow started falling, and continued to fall through December 25. Winds picked up and whipped snow into massive drifts over highways, cars, houses, and the airport. About 23–29 inches of snow fell during the Blizzard of 1982, bringing Denver and its surrounding suburbs to a near standstill. Maintenance crews eventually had to give up trying to keep even one runway clear, and the airport closed until December 26. (Courtesy of DEN.)

By 1985, Stapleton was heavily congested and had one of the worst records in the United States for runway closings and flight delays due to bad weather. Denver was losing passengers, and the money they brought with them, to Salt Lake City. Bill Franklin, vice president of the Denver Chamber of Commerce, said at the time, "Airports are probably the highest and most important priority companies have when they look for a place to grow. In terms of economic development, whether you look at high tech or a regional headquarters, access to good air transportation is certainly one of their most important considerations." (Courtesy of DEN.)

This photograph shows the full buildout of Stapleton's runway configuration. The next step was to expand northeast into the Rocky Mountain Arsenal. Adams County, which owned the Arsenal land, threatened a lawsuit to stop the expansion. When Mayor Federico Peña was elected in 1980, he reversed the push to annex the land and began negotiations with Adams County to instead build a new airport much farther east. (Courtesy of DEN.)

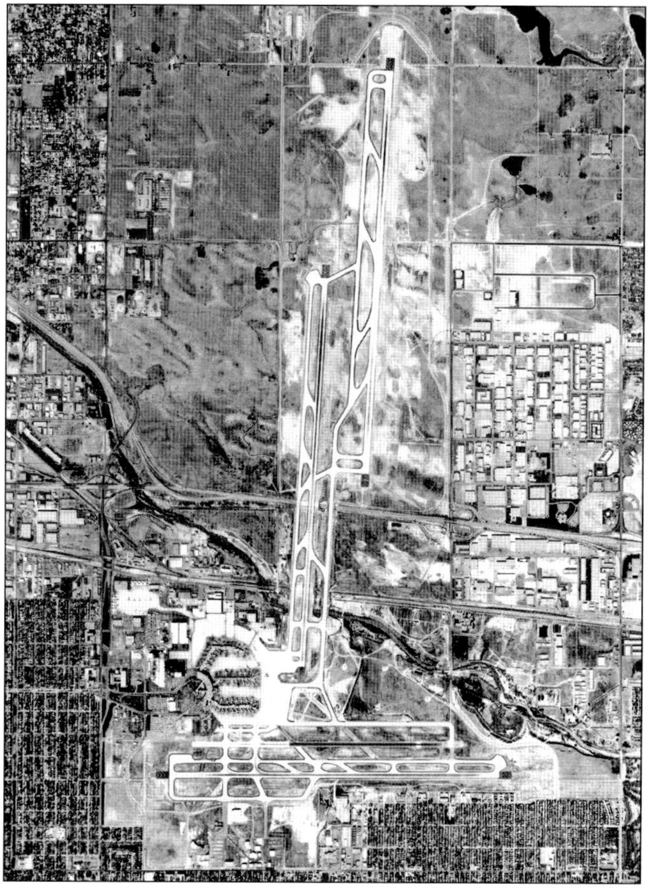

By 1983, Denver was the most over-served market in the country. United, Continental, and Frontier traditionally fought for market dominance at Stapleton, but deregulation brought new air carriers and expanded operations for others to the Denver market including Delta, American, Eastern, Northwest, Piedmont, and Southwest. (Courtesy of DEN.)

Continental Airlines CEO Robert F. Six retired in 1978. Alvin L. Feldman took over the airline but struggled to establish a two-hub system based in Denver and Houston, with wide-bodied aircraft ill-suited to the new hub and spoke model. Continental started the era of deregulation with the fourth-strongest airline balance sheet but was in bankruptcy within five years. After Feldman's untimely death, Texas International CEO Frank Lorenzo acquired the airline, taking the company into bankruptcy, cutting staff, and turning the airline into a low-cost carrier. (Courtesy of DEN.)

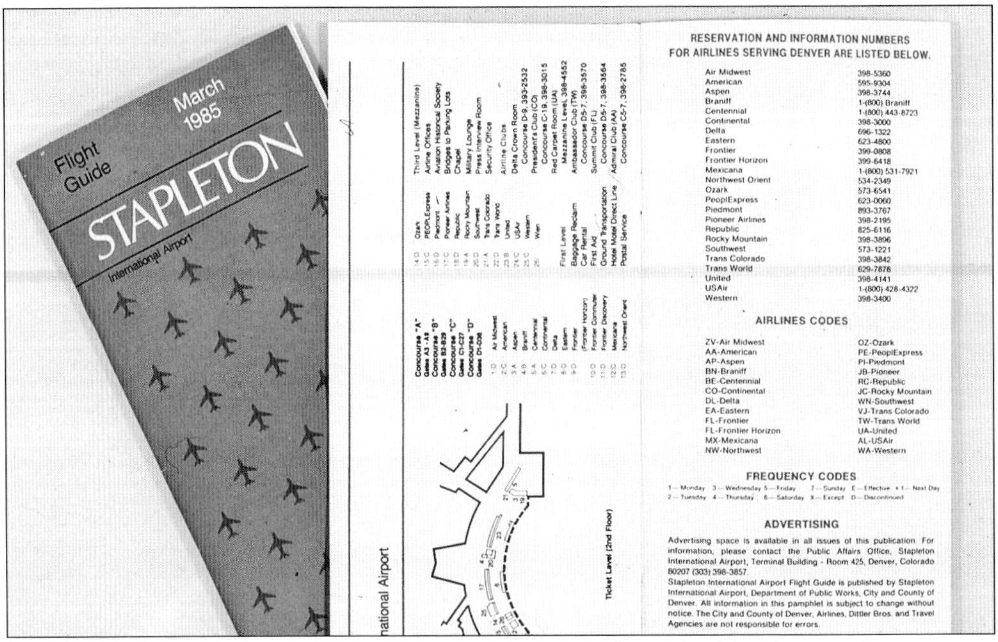

This 1985 flight guide to Stapleton International Airport shows the 24 airlines with service out of the airport at the time, but the list was about to change. After acquiring Continental, Frank Lorenzo acquired People Express, Frontier, and New York Air, along with several commuters to create the third-largest airline in the United States. He was trying to acquire Eastern Airlines when Continental was sold to Scandinavian Airlines Systems. (Courtesy of DEN.)

This view of concourse D shows the dominance of Frontier Airlines at Stapleton. However, Frontier was the next domino to fall in the deregulation era. As airfares plummeted, the airlines played a game of attrition—whoever could suffer losses the longest would win. Frontier was sold to People Express in 1985, which was bought by Frank Lorenzo's new Continental Airlines when People Express closed its doors in August 1986. People Express and Frontier were all rolled into the Continental fleet. (Courtesy of CHS.)

With deregulation, new airlines such as America West, Midway, and People Express were formed. The People Express model was low-fare and no-frills. However, as the airline expanded it found its competitors matching its low fares. Competitors were also gaining passengers who did not like having to pay extra for food and checked bags on People Express. People Express purchased Frontier Airlines and implemented its no-frills model, but the reaction from many loyal Frontier passengers was to avoid flying both airlines. (Photograph by Jeffrey Price.)

Deregulation also had an effect on the commuter and regional airlines. Aspen Airways provided low-cost trips from Stapleton to destinations throughout Colorado and the region. In 1985, a passenger could pay just $32 to fly from Stapleton to Aspen, Colorado, without making advance reservations. This photograph shows three of the Convair 580s on the A+ concourse ramp at Stapleton. By 1989, Aspen was up for sale, with its assets purchased by Mesa, Air Wisconsin, and other carriers. (Photograph by Jeffrey Price.)

Rocky Mountain Airways was another victim of the deregulation era. Formed in 1966 as Vail Airways, the carrier relied heavily on seasonal ski tourist traffic and put the first de Havilland DHC-7-102 ("Dash 7") into service. Its short takeoff and landing capabilities were well suited to the mountain resorts. Texas Air bought Rocky Mountain in 1986 and began flying as Continental Express. The Dash 7 in this photograph still bears its Rocky Mountain Airways livery, although the name had been changed to Continental Express. (Courtesy of DEN.)

Changes in the airline industry also resulted in changes to the choice of aircraft they used. Here, a United Airlines Boeing 727 taxis over Interstate 70. One of the last aircraft in service into the late 1990s with more than two engines, the three-engine aircraft was less fuel efficient, noisier, and required a third crew member, the flight engineer, which kept operating costs higher than the newer two-engine, two-pilot aircraft. (Photograph by Zig Price.)

In 1983, Colorado governor Richard Lamm (center left) cuts the ribbon with Southwest Airlines CEO Herb Kelleher (center right) to officially welcome the airline to Stapleton. The run would be short-lived, however, with Southwest leaving just two years later and not returning to the Denver market until 2006. The carrier opposed Denver International Airport and cited high operating costs as the reason for its departure. (Courtesy of Southwest Airlines.)

The 1980s were a tumultuous time in the aviation industry, with numerous bombings, hijackings, and other acts of air terror throughout the world. Between 1985 and 1989, two significant bombings, Pan Am Flight 103 and UTA Flight 772; the hijacking of TWA 847; and the downing of PSA Flight 1771 would bring a renewed focus on securing air travel. This photograph shows passengers walking through a screening checkpoint at Stapleton. At the time, airline contractors conducted passenger and carry-on bag screening. (Courtesy of DEN.)

By 1986, plans were underway for the construction of a new concourse, new taxiways, and a runway for the north air-cargo operation (top left); modifications to the A+ commuter airline concourse; and other improvements. This graphic also shows a potential connection (top right) to Rocky Mountain Arsenal land as the decision had not yet been made whether to expand to Arsenal land or relocate the airport. (Courtesy of DEN.)

In an attempt to accommodate the new passenger traffic, Stapleton opened up 24 gates on the newly constructed concourse E. Concourse E would only be used for a little under 10 years, but with the overcapacity issues, the new gates and ramp space were necessary. The image above shows part of the construction of the concourse, which opened in 1988, and the interior photograph below shows the new perspective on terminal design, focusing more on open space and aesthetics rather than just function. (Both, courtesy of DEN.)

Passengers walk through Stapleton's great hall in the main terminal in the 1980s. (Courtesy of DEN.)

This Curtis Jenny used to hang in the terminal building at Stapleton International Airport. The Jenny was considered the Model T of the skies, and aviation legend Elrey Jeppesen's first flight was in the JN-4 Jenny. It was relocated to Denver International Airport. (Courtesy of DEN.)

The design of the original tower at Stapleton included a large hotel with the tower cab sitting on top. Later designs included a restaurant at the base of the tower, but the concept was never realized. This photograph shows air-traffic controller Larry Bell staffing a position in the tower. (Courtesy of CHS.)

A UPS DC-8 is shown taxiing at Stapleton. UPS, founded in 1907, handles nearly 18 million packages each day, operating over 200 aircraft serving over 300 destinations daily. At Stapleton, air-cargo operations were relegated to the north cargo ramp known as Northfield, located just northwest of Interstate 70, but the cargo companies would play a significant role in the design of Denver International Airport. (Courtesy of DEN.)

Stapleton's capacity issues were not limited to the airfield. Vehicle access to the airport was also becoming increasingly congested. Shown here are the airport's four-story parking garage (right) and passenger pick-up and drop-off lanes. (Courtesy of DEN.)

On November 25, 1990, fire broke out at Stapleton's fuel farm. After two days, firefighters were unable to extinguish the flaming fuel. Large tank fire contractors arrived and put the fire out in 45 minutes. Seven of the twelve fuel storage tanks were burned or damaged and the fire consumed over 1.6 million gallons of fuel. Over 600 firefighters, 47 airport and city fire units, and 4 contract personnel were engaged in the fire, using 56 million gallons of water and 28,000 gallons of foam. About $15–$20 million in losses were suffered. (Courtesy of DEN.)

Named in honor of Continental's founder, the Robert F. Six Continental Airlines flight reservation center occupied the north side of Stapleton for many years but was eventually relocated to Houston, Texas. Before the advent of the Internet, reservation agents and travel agents were the predominant means of booking a flight. (Courtesy of Barb Swarts.)

The 94th Aero Squadron was a World War I–themed restaurant located east of the east-west runway complex. Sitting only a few hundred yards from runway 8R/26L, its large windows and outdoor seating afforded front row views of aircraft taking off and landing at Stapleton. The French chateau theme featured pictures and artifacts of the time, and guests could put on earphones and listen in on Denver's actual air-traffic control communications. The restaurant burned down in 1990 due to an electrical fire. (Photograph by Jeffrey Price.)

In its final two years of operation, Stapleton receive another distinguished visitor when Pope John Paul II came to Denver for World Youth Day in 1993. The photograph above shows the pope arriving on Alitalia to a waiting security contingent. (Above, courtesy of DEN; below, courtesy of Jennifer Price.)

By 1990, Stapleton International Airport was fully built out with six concourses and five runways. The airport was over capacity, and the ground was already broken for construction of Denver International Airport. The projected opening date was just a couple of years off, but with baggage system problems and other delays, Stapleton would have to hold on for a few more years than anticipated. (Courtesy of DEN.)

Stapleton International Airport closed on February 27, 1995. A single radio call went out from the airport operations manager on duty, notifying pilots that the airport was now permanently closed. The aircraft had already departed, and the caravans of ground vehicles were long gone. After slightly over 65 years of service, Stapleton's purpose had been served. Ironically, current FAA regulations call for airline pilots to also retire at 65 years. (Photograph by Zig Price.)

Taken just a few days after closing, this photograph shows the abandoned and empty terminal building and ramp areas that were left behind. To the left is concourse B and the air-traffic control tower. (Courtesy of DEN.)

Shortly after closing, developers began to disassemble Stapleton. This photograph shows the site of concourse E, just eight years after its commissioning. Today, a large mixed-use residential community sits on the site of the former airport. The tower was the only structure left standing and is the site of a new restaurant. A long park now winds through the subdivisions where the former east-west runway complex used to be. (Courtesy of DEN.)

Four

Building the Field of Dreams

If You Build It, Will They Come?

It was called the field of dreams. Denver International Airport was the mega-project that was not supposed to succeed, yet despite all obstacles, today stands as one of the busiest airports in the world, exceeding all previous passenger projects and in record time. The airport is a huge economic generator for the Denver metropolitan area. Denver mayor Federico Peña played the decisive role by deciding to build a new airport instead of expanding the existing Stapleton airport and got the project in motion, notwithstanding the numerous problems that came in the years that followed. Elected in 1983, Peña was the first Hispanic mayor of Denver. He was re-elected in 1987 on a platform of heavy campaigning for a new airport; however, the project would still need the support of voters in both Adams and Denver Counties. This photograph shows concourse C and the FAA control tower being constructed in the early 1990s. (Courtesy of DEN.)

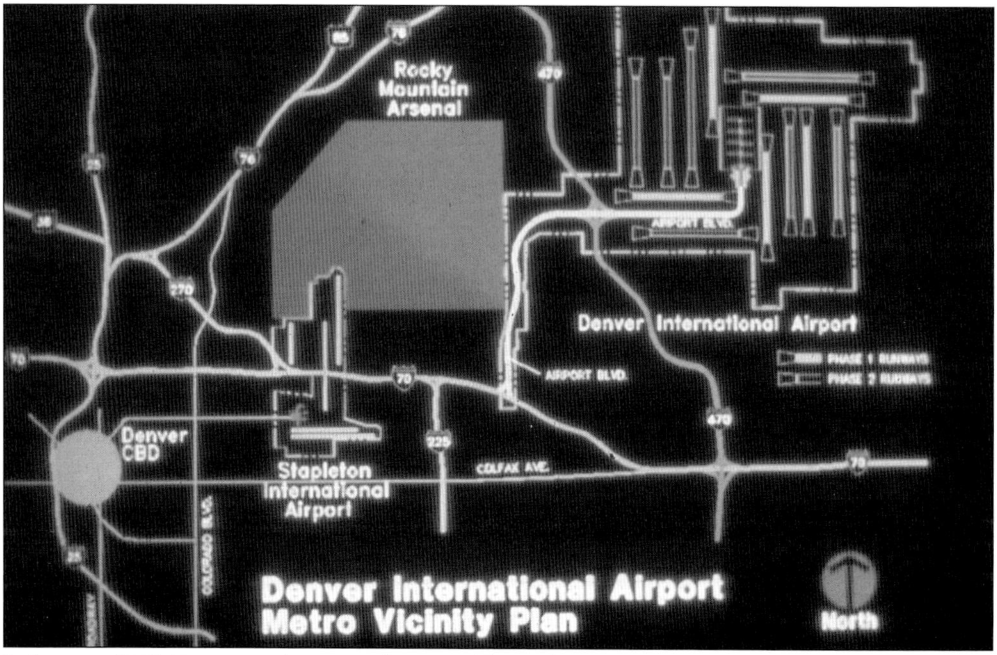

In January 1985, Denver and its next-door neighbor Adams County reached an agreement to build the new airport on land east of the Rocky Mountain Arsenal. Various locations were considered, and the final location was still criticized for being too far away from the city, which was the same argument that opponents made when the Sand Creek site was selected to build the Denver Municipal Airport in 1929. DIA's location, at 24 miles from Denver's central business district, makes it one of the most remote airports in the world. (Courtesy of DEN.)

Hoping to avoid the noise complaints from the homes near Stapleton and allow for future expansion, the city annexed 53 square miles of what was mostly farmland from Adams County. The surrounding land was then home to the Arrowhead and Eastwood Estates mobile home parks, which had to be acquired by the city, and previously, Denver International Raceway, one of Colorado's oldest drag racing strips. (Courtesy of DEN.)

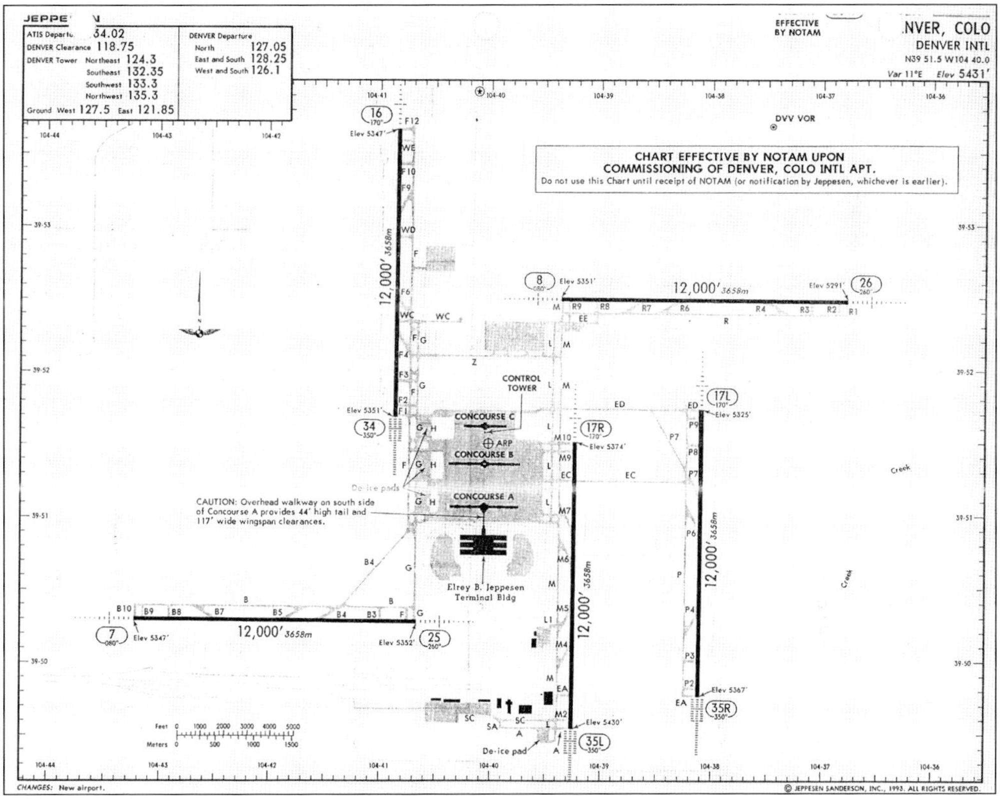

Runway location is the foundation of all airport planning. Airport planners attempt to design a runway system that is safe, efficient, expandable, and reduces noise to the surrounding community. A key condition is that the configuration should allow two runways to be available for landing at all times. While Denver had chosen an L-shaped configuration similar to Stapleton's, the FAA preferred the pinwheel concept, shown here in its final form. (Courtesy of Jeppesen Charts.)

Fentress Bradburn Architects designed the terminal and DIA's iconic tent roof. Terminal design should focus on the efficient movement of passengers, aircraft, and baggage, and the ability to easily transfer passengers between flights. To achieve efficient aircraft movement required the concourses to be separated far enough to allow plenty of maneuvering room for airplane push back and taxiing. (Courtesy of DEN.)

DIA's predecessor, Stapleton, experienced plenty of congestion between the B and C concourses as aircraft size increased, something DIA planners wanted to avoid. Fentress planners felt that the best design was to put the concourses mid-field, connected by an underground train system. This would allow aircraft to park on both sides of the concourses, and reduce passenger walking distances. (Courtesy of DEN.)

This 1994 photograph shows the completed runway 25. On the left is the rental car facility under construction. The yellow "X" painted over the runway number tells pilots that the runway is currently closed. The X is removed when the runway is ready for operation. Compared to Stapleton's one 12,000-foot runway, all five of DIA's initial runways were built to accommodate the largest airliners at the time, including the Airbus A380. Each runway is 12,000 feet in length and 150 feet wide. (Courtesy of DEN.)

Originally, the rental car area, shown here, was designated for level 1 of the parking garages, and constructed so it did not access levels 2 through 5. However, rental car agencies preferred a 150-acre tract along Peña Boulevard and did not want to pay the fees for the garage operation. The decision to move the rental cars was a blessing in disguise, as the alternate baggage system would eat up a lot of garage parking, much of which could be made up with the level 1 spaces. (Courtesy of DEN.)

The air-cargo facility was originally located on the north side of the airfield, but cargo operators complained it was too far away from Interstate 70. Nearby Front Range Airport, a small general aviation airport just east of DIA, offered to accommodate all of the cargo operators. Although Denver had already graded the north cargo location, under threat of losing the cargo companies completely, the cargo facility was moved to the south side of DIA. (Courtesy of DEN.)

This is an excellent view of the terminal building as it starts to come together. In the center, slightly to the left, is the Airport Office Building. Concourse C and the FAA tower are largely complete at this point, concourse B construction is well underway, and construction on concourse A is just getting started. (Courtesy of DEN.)

Curtis Fentress said, "I envisioned a rejuvenation of the airport building through the incorporation of great spaces, along the lines of what took place with Grand Central Station. Passengers, the world over, are asking for airports to become more than people processors. I have found an opportunity to transfix the wonder and excitement of flight in the architecture of airport." (Courtesy of DEN.)

Personnel construct a screening checkpoint inside the main terminal. Since DIA was designed before the terrorist attacks on September 11, 2001, screening checkpoints did not have to take up too much floor space. Post-9/11 checkpoint designs would prompt Denver to begin planning to relocate its security screening areas to be less exposed to the public. (Courtesy of DEN.)

Due to the vast distances between concourses, the underground train system is essential to the airport. The Automated Guideway Transit System operates on either side of the terminal, carrying up to 6,000 passengers per hour at a speed of 30 miles per hour. Initial passenger loads exceeded estimates, and additional cars and entry/exit locations had to be added. (Courtesy of DEN.)

Denver International Airport's Art and Culture Program administers the City and County of Denver's "one percent for art" ordinance, which requires one percent of the budget of a city project to be allocated to artwork. In the center of concourse B, the "Beaded Circle Crossing" spans a moving walkway and was created with the lodges, tipis, and beadwork of Native Americans in mind and the bridges of Gustave Eiffel and Santiago Calatrava. (Photograph by Jeffrey Price.)

An unfortunate part of DIA's legacy is the baggage system. Typical "tug and cart" methods were considered too slow for the vast distances between DIA's terminal and the concourses, and United Airlines would only agree to constructing DIA if the city built a state-of-the-art automated baggage system. The new system used a cart for each piece of luggage launched down a series of tracks out to the concourse. (Courtesy of DEN.)

The automated baggage system was supposed to use 3,100 small carts for normal sized luggage and 450 large carts for skis, golf clubs, and other oversized items. The carts would travel at 17 miles per hour, and move 700 bags per minute. Below, Denver's director of aviation, Ginger Evans, a top engineer brought on board to get DIA's construction schedule back on track, talks with contractors about the baggage system. The system was cutting edge but had never been attempted on the scale and complexity that DIA required. Denver eventually used portions of the east and west level 3 parking garages to construct a new "alternate" baggage sorting area, where bags would be loaded on carts and tugged out to the concourse "old-school" style. This alternate system was supposed to be temporary until the automated system was up and running, but by 2005, the automated system was removed and sold for scrap. (Both, courtesy of DEN.)

DIA was based on the premise that its three hubbing carriers—United, Continental, and Frontier—would continue to base at the new airport. But by 1990, Frontier was gone and Continental was cutting back flight operations out of Denver. Continental did not completely trust that the underground train system would always work, and with no alternative for passengers to walk to the concourses, would only agree to the DIA deal if the airport constructed a bridge from the terminal to its operation on concourse A. In his final days as CEO of Continental, Frank Lorenzo signed an agreement to base at DIA on concourse A. (Courtesy of DEN.)

This photograph shows the view from the FAA control tower facing southwest, providing a commanding view of the airfield. (Courtesy of DEN.)

In the months leading up to opening day, the airport held numerous events to get future passengers used to the new facility, including bike races on the ramp, VIP dinners in the terminal, public open houses, and the Denver International Air Show. This photograph, taken in September 1993, shows the F-117 Stealth Fighter. The air show also featured the USAF Thunderbirds, the US Army's Golden Knights, the Royal Air Force Red Arrows, and the Canadian Snowbirds. (Courtesy of DEN.)

DIA's main terminal's Teflon-coated fiberglass roof is not only one of the first striking images visitors to Denver see, but also allows in vast amounts of natural light. It is designed to shed snow and, if gets too heavy, to tear at the edges first to channel the snow and water rather than collapse in the center. The roof's unique design is able to reflect sunlight during summer months and retain heat during the winter, saving costs on air conditioning and heating. (Photograph by Zig Price.)

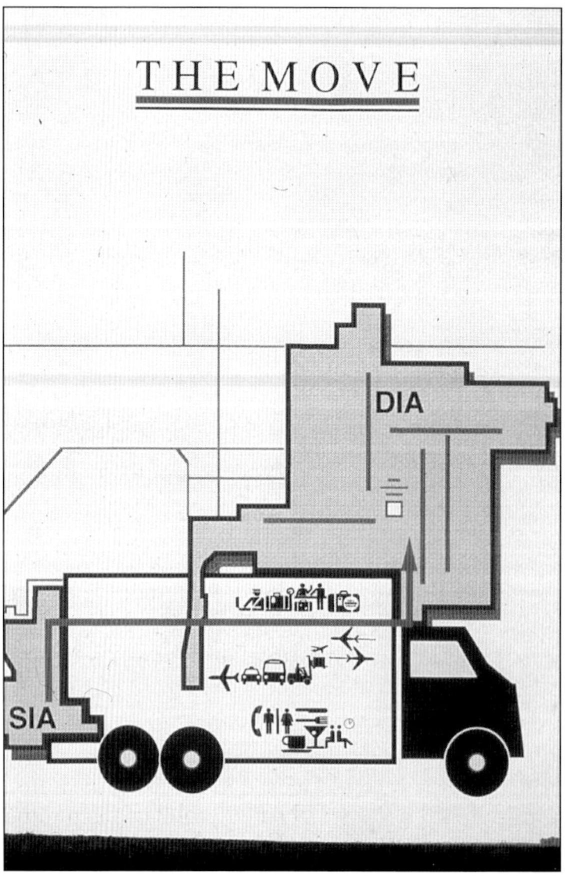

This rare photograph of concourse C, as seen from the concourse B ramp control tower, shows the airport shortly before any air traffic used it. After two previous opening-day delays, the terminal and the airfield at Denver International Airport were finally ready for business. But first, everything from Stapleton had to be moved. (Photograph by Zig Price.)

It was called Push Night. As a winter storm made its way toward Denver, airport personnel, the airlines, contractors, vendors, and tenants all made their way from Stapleton International Airport to Denver International Airport. This graphic was the cover of the comprehensive plan for the move. Over 1,400 relocation action items had to be worked out by 27 management teams, all while keeping one airport operational and preparing to open another one. (Courtesy of DEN.)

Noncritical equipment had been hauled to the new airport for many months prior, but approximately 50 percent of the equipment necessary to operate DIA needed to remain at Stapleton right up until Push Night. Everything needed to get to DIA within an 18-hour window. Side streets were closed as caravans of tugs, trucks, 18-wheelers, and all other sorts of airport equipment moved toward their new home (Courtesy of DEN.)

While vehicles slowly made their way to the new airport, inside DIA, airport operations and security personnel were scrambling to ensure the airport would meet FAA security measures. All concourses beyond the screening checkpoints had to be searched for prohibited items and personnel (called sterilizing) before the airport could open to the public. Reporters chased nearly anyone with a possible story to tell. (Courtesy of DEN.)

As the storm moved in, the seemingly endless caravans of airport vehicles continued to DIA. Stapleton's east-west runway complex was closed at 1:00 p.m., and the Push started 30 minutes later. The long, slow-moving line of vehicles paraded through Gate 49, along Havana Street on the east side of the airport, north on Havana to Fifty-Sixth Avenue, then out to DIA. Emergency shelter stations with coffee and first-aid kits were set up along the route, and by late afternoon, the freezing rain and snow had settled in. (Courtesy of DEN.)

United Flight 1062 to Kansas City was the first departure from DIA, with 300 passengers departing at 6:00 a.m. United Flight 1474 was the first arrival, carrying 128 passengers from Colorado Springs, arriving shortly after the first departure, a few minutes late. Aircraft continued to land at a rate of 92 per hour during peak traffic, compared to the 32 per hour that Stapleton could have handled during the snowstorm. It has been said that DIA opened during the kind of snowstorm that would have closed Stapleton. Here, a United 737 departs on a clear day. (Courtesy of DEN.)

Mayor Wellington Webb, who took over the massive DIA project and saw it through to completion, is shown here speaking on opening day: "There are some this morning that hoped we would not be successful. Now what we must collectively do is bind our hands together and market this facility for this city, the metropolitan area, the state and this nation." (Courtesy of DEN.)

Denver International Airport director of aviation Jim Delong stands at the opening ceremony holding an enlarged copy of the Airport Operating Certificate. The FAA issues this certificate, which authorizes an airport to conduct commercial operations. (Courtesy of DEN.)

Denver's mayor and secretary of transportation under the Clinton administration Federico Peña speaks at the opening of the airport that he envisioned: "If you're going to make courageous decisions, you've got to take strategic risks. The critics don't build great cities." The 11-mile stretch of road, Peña Boulevard, which leads from Interstate 70 to the airport, is named after him. When Mayor Stapleton envisioned a new airport for Denver, some in the press called it "Stapleton's Folly." When Mayor Peña envisioned a new airport for the city, some in the press called it "Federico's Folly." Denver's first airport, Denver Municipal Airport, declared that the city intended to be a player in the new world of aviation. Stapleton International Airport brought the city into the jet age and through the ups and downs of the deregulated airline industry. Denver International Airport is now a crown jewel in the worldwide airport system and is poised to continue meeting the needs of the traveling public far into the future. (Courtesy of DEN.)

Five

Denver International Airport

Proving the Critics Wrong Once Again

Elrey Jeppesen is considered the founder of the modern aeronautical chart. An early airmail pilot at a time when most pilots relied on road maps, railroad tracks, and known landmarks along the way, Jeppesen would take notes about the obstacles and safe paths into and out of airports. Word spread throughout the pilot community, and soon, it seemed that all of the pilots wanted copies of his "Little Black Book." Jeppesen founded his own company to produce his charts, which are still in production. Jeppesen passed away in 1996, but lived long enough to see the terminal at Denver International Airport named in his honor. This Jeppesen bronze statue stands tall in the great hall of DIA. (Photograph by Jeffrey Price.)

Another aviation pioneer honored at Denver International Airport is cable TV magnate Bill Daniels. In addition to his many other endeavors, which included owning part of the Los Angeles Lakers basketball team, Daniels and a crew of four piloted a Learjet 35A around the world, at an average speed of 463.5 mph, setting a world speed record for business jets. Today, it hangs from the ceiling in concourse C. Daniels passed away in 2000. (Courtesy of Jeffrey Price.)

Several of DIA's paintings and artwork have been the subject of controversy, but none more so than the work of painter Leo Tanguma. His murals "In Peace and Harmony with Nature" and "Children of the World Dream of Peace" adorn the walls of the Jeppesen terminal and have long been at the center of conspiracy theories because of their eclectic blend of imagery. (Photograph by Jeffrey Price.)

In this 1999 photograph, artist Marcus Akinlana paints "Mile High and Rising" as part of the A Cultural Perspective Project. It depicts the spirit of adventure, optimism, and triumph that African Americans brought to Colorado and the Old West, featuring historical figures like Barney Ford and "Aunt Clara" Brown. (Courtesy of DEN.)

Shortly after the opening of Denver International Airport, United Airlines was clearly the dominant carrier, and by 1996, United and its code-sharing partners commanded a 78 percent share of the market. Continental Airlines was reducing flights to Denver, and other low fare airlines were either being absorbed, as Morris Air was by Southwest, or stopping service, as Midway Airlines did between Denver and Chicago. MarkAir shut down, and GP Express (formerly Continental Express) closed its doors, which eliminated several Rocky Mountain ski resort destinations. (Courtesy of DEN.)

In 1994, a group of original Frontier Airline executives reincarnated the former airline. At first, Frontier served several secondary markets such as Albuquerque, New Mexico; Billings, Montana; and El Paso, Texas. Frontier also served Las Vegas, Nevada, and would soon add Los Angeles International Airport, Orlando International Airport, LaGuardia Airport, and Reagan/National Airport. The Denver-based carrier's presence helped lower airfares on numerous routes and brought a hometown airline back to Denver. (Photograph by Shahn Sederberg.)

While airlines were shutting down at Denver International, new competition emerged from the Colorado Springs Regional Airport in the form of Western Pacific Airlines. WestPac started in April 1995, with flights from Colorado Springs to Los Angeles, Las Vegas, and Oklahoma City. WestPac's 737s were easily identifiable on the airport with their characteristic "flying billboard" livery. After two years of not making a profit, new management moved WestPac to Denver International and attempted a merger with the new Frontier Airlines. The merger and WestPac would both fail, with WestPac declaring bankruptcy in 1998. (Courtesy of DEN.)

In 1997, a unique airplane made a visit to DIA, the supersonic Concorde. The visit was part of the Denver Economic Summit of the Eight (G8), which brought together world leaders from the United States, Canada, Japan, Britain, France, Germany, Italy, and Russia to weigh global economic issues. The Concorde had visited Stapleton in 1978, but due to a prohibition against commercial aircraft traveling at supersonic speeds, it was never cost effective to fly the plane over the US mainland. (Courtesy of DEN.)

The Summit was originally called the G7, but when Russian president Boris Yeltsin (pictured) accepted an invitation, it became the Summit of the Eight. Numerous aircraft from all the represented nations arrived into Denver International Airport and parked on the west side deicing areas. Security was very tight for the foreign dignitaries who all stopped for a quick reception on the airport tarmac before heading to meetings in downtown Denver. (Courtesy of DEN.)

Pres. Bill Clinton arrives at Denver International Airport to be part of the Economic Summit of the Eight in 1993. (Courtesy of DEN.)

Some questioned the location of Denver International Airport due to the potential for more violent weather than Stapleton typically experienced. While Colorado experiences fewer and less violent tornadoes than most other tornado-alley states, such as Kansas, Oklahoma, and Nebraska, both Stapleton and DIA have occasionally had to suspend flight operations due to a funnel cloud or tornado. The National Center for Atmospheric Research's 1992 *Bulletin of the American Meteorological Society* noted that meteorologists and aviation experts have concluded that DIA's location does not raise special concerns regarding weather safety. (Courtesy of DEN.)

DIA was billed as an all-weather airport and, with the exception of a blizzard in the fall of 1997, almost never faced a storm it couldn't handle. However, in December 2006, a blizzard struck the Denver area dropping 25 inches of snow that brought both air and ground travel to a halt. The storm stranded over 4,700 passengers, along with many airport and airline employees who could not make it through the impassable conditions. (Photograph by Jeffrey Price.)

The blizzard of 2006 was a warning that the airport needed to be better equipped to handle the big storms. The airport hired a consultant to revise its snow and ice control plan, and purchased multifunction equipment (MFE) that can plow, sweep, and blow snow at the same time. MFEs are common at airports that receive large amounts of annual snowfall. Denver maintains 250 pieces of airside snow removal equipment and 120 pieces of equipment for landside parking lots and roadways. A standard snow blower is shown in this photograph. (Courtesy of DEN.)

In 1987, Continental Flight 1713 crashed on takeoff from Stapleton International Airport, killing 28 people. The National Transportation Safety Board concluded that too much time elapsed between aircraft deicing and takeoff. DIA's deicing pads are as close to the runways as possible to reduce the time between deicing and taking off. DIA has five centralized deice pads with 27 deicing spaces. Propylene Glycol (deicing fluid) is collected as the glycol runs off the airplane and is recycled into windshield washer fluid and other consumer products. This photograph shows an American Airlines airplane at DIA being deiced. (Courtesy of DEN.)

The Aircraft Rescue and Fire Fighting (ARFF) capabilities at DIA exceed the FAA standard for a commercial service airport. With seven crash response fire trucks, each valued at an estimated $1.3 million, DIA is considered a leader in disaster preparedness. Four ARFF fire stations located throughout the airfield ensure a rapid response to nearly any location at the airport within minutes. DIA opened a fifth station in 2017 and can respond with a variety of vehicles, from rapid intervention vehicles to smaller trucks that can respond in the airport parking garages, to structural trucks for building fires. (Courtesy of Shahn Sederberg.)

Denver International Airport has a complete state-of-the-art Aircraft Rescue and Fire Fighting Academy on site, with a 75-foot aircraft live-fire training simulator. The simulator can recreate aircraft interior and exterior fires, and fuel spill fires. Two actual Swearingen SA226s (regional airplanes) are available for training in various types of scenarios. (Courtesy of Shahn Sederberg.)

An F-16 from the 120th Fighter Squadron at Buckley Air Force Base, which is part of the 140th Wing, Colorado Air National Guard, sits on the ramp at Denver International Airport. The runway at Buckley was undergoing maintenance, and the F-16 squadron temporarily relocated to DIA in order to maintain mission readiness. (Courtesy of DEN.)

The most common disruption to flight operations is typically weather or air-traffic control congestion, but on September 11, 2001, the United States experienced an incident far worse than a blizzard or thunderstorm. When terrorists crashed two hijacked aircraft (American Airlines Flight 11 and United Airlines Flight 175) into the World Trade Center in New York, another hijacked jet (American Airlines Flight 77) into the Pentagon, and a fourth hijacked jet (United Airlines Flight 93) into a field in Pennsylvania, for the first time in the history of aviation, the FAA ordered the grounding of all civil aircraft in the United States. (Photograph by Jeannette Hilaire.)

Taken on September 11, this photograph shows an airport Emergency Response Team (ERT) member helping passengers find their way back out of the airport. The DIA ERT program uses volunteers who already work at the airport in other capacities to don a vest and assist during large-scale incidents and emergencies. With the exception of military flights and certain aircraft involved in firefighting operations in California, US airspace was shut down for two days. (Photograph by Jeannette Hilaire.)

When the airspace reopened on September 13, 2001, a new set of security rules were put into place. Throughout the United States, the new rules created up to four-plus-hour lines at screening checkpoints. This photograph shows only part of the lines that formed at DIA. The screening process and how aviation views terrorism and security were forever changed. (Courtesy of DEN.)

Within two months of the terrorist attacks, a new agency had been formed, the Transportation Security Administration (TSA). In the next year, TSA took over passenger and carry-on baggage screening from the airline contractors, started screening checked baggage for the first time in the United States, and took over enforcement of airport and air carrier security programs. In 2003, TSA was moved under the newly created Department of Homeland Security. (Photograph by Jeffrey Price.)

Safety is always first at any airport, but incidents still happen. In 1997, this B-727 struck an employee shuttle bus that had failed to yield to the plane while it was crossing the cargo ramp. The copilot suffered non–life threatening injuries, and the airport immediately implemented procedures to ensure the accident would not be repeated. (Photograph by Jeffrey Price.)

Behind the scenes of Denver International Airport, a dedicated crew works to ensure the safety, security, and efficiency of flight operations. In this image, operations manager Mike Carlson coordinates a presidential arrival. Airport operations personnel are responsible for solving any problem and facilitating whatever process is necessary to keep passengers and planes moving. Their duties are wide-ranging, from coordinating a visit from Air Force One, to responding to an airfield emergency, directing snow removal operations, or handling a security incident, all of which—and more—can happen in one shift. (Courtesy of DEN.)

Airport maintenance personnel are critical to the function of the airport, working to ensure the facilities, vehicle fleets, and the airfield are prepared for service. In addition to the 50,000-plus employees who work at DIA for the airlines, tenants, vendors, contractors, and various federal agencies, DIA employs thousands of its own staff to administrate and operate the airport. Above is part of DIA's snowplow fleet. Below, from left to right, airport noise abatement officers Mike McKee, Michelle Bartholomew, and Jeannette Hilaire analyze flight track information. (Both, courtesy of DEN.)

Airport police and the FBI conduct a hijack exercise at Denver International Airport. A large contingent of Denver police and security officers patrol the airport on a daily basis and respond to incidents at the airport. (Photograph by Jeffrey Price.)

When DIA first opened, a fountain occupied the center of the terminal where passengers come up from the train system, returning from the concourse areas. The fountain turned out to be too loud and was eventually replaced with lounge areas and occasional art exhibits. (Courtesy of DEN.)

Southwest Airlines officially returned to the Denver market in 2006 and now holds a principal position at the airport, with an average of 200 flights a day. The airline has retained its popularity with travelers due its friendly nature and generally lower fares. (Both, photographs by Shahn Sederberg.)

America West Airlines started operations in 1983, after the passage of the Airline Deregulation Act in 1978. America West was one of the first airlines to use cross-utilization. America West employees were trained in a variety of jobs, such as pilots cross-trained as dispatchers and baggage handlers and flight attendants cross-trained as gate agents. The airline operated through bankruptcy between 1991 and 1994, eventually reemerging with new livery and a new online reservation system. America West merged with US Airways in 2005. US Airways has a long history in the aviation industry, going back to 1939. Up until 1979, the airline was better known as Allegheny Airlines, changing its name after deregulation to USAir. USAir bought Pacific Southwest Airlines and Piedmont Airlines in the late 1980s, and expanded its service to Europe with flights to London, Paris, and Frankfurt. It rebranded as US Airways in 1997, and eventually merged with America West. US Airways then later merged with American Airlines in 2013. (Above, photograph by Jeffrey Price; below, courtesy of DEN.)

A Northwest Airlines B-727 is seen above taking off from Denver International Airport in the mid-1990s. Northwest was founded in 1926 and at one point was ranked the sixth largest airline in domestic and international scheduled passenger miles flown. Regional flights operated under Mesaba Airlines, Pinnacle Airlines, and Compass Airlines. Northwest started cutting back in early 2001, but following the September 11 attacks, the company laid off numerous employees and took other cost-cutting measures. In 2008, Northwest merged with American Airlines. (Both, courtesy of DEN.)

The new Frontier Airlines would experience problems by 2008, when it filed for Chapter 11 bankruptcy in reaction to the intent of its credit card processor, First Data, to withhold significant proceeds from ticket sales. Republic Airways Holdings acquired Frontier and its regional airline, Lynx Aviation, during a bankruptcy auction in 2009. In 2013, Republic sold Frontier to Indigo Partners, which turned the company into an ultra–low cost airline and continued to hub at Denver International Airport. (Photograph by Jeffrey Price.)

For many years, the pioneers on foot, horse, or wagon, followed by the railroads and even the air mail routes, avoided traveling west through Denver due to the daunting Rocky Mountains. International air carriers have also been hesitant to fly non-stop to Denver from overseas. Local industry and tourism, plus advancements in aircraft design leading to better fuel efficiency and better performance at higher altitudes, means Denver is now well within reach of numerous foreign countries. Korean Air, Lufthansa, British Airways, Icelandair, and Aeromexico are among the international carriers at DIA, along with several international air-cargo operators. This photograph shows a Korean Air B-747 taxiing into the gate on concourse A at DIA. (Courtesy of DEN.)

Continental Air Lines was founded in 1934 and, along with United Air Lines, was one of the two first hubbing airlines at Stapleton International Airport. A more complete history of Continental is told in earlier chapters, but by 2010, the airline continued to expand particularly on international routes, and became the first airline to launch a mobile boarding pass service, allowing customers to receive boarding passes electronically on their mobile phones. Continental merged with United Airlines in 2010, using the United name but putting the Continental logo on the tail of all of its aircraft. (Above, courtesy of DEN; below, courtesy of Shahn Sederberg.)

In the early days of the Stapleton airport, much of the revenue came from the private aircraft flight operations. However, when Denver International Airport opened, most of the general aviation traffic relocated to one of the three general aviation airports in the Denver metro area. DIA still conducts about 5,000-plus general aviation operations per year. In this photograph, a Citation X, the world's fastest business jet, sits on the ramp at DIA. (Courtesy of DEN.)

Fred Smith changed the world with a concept of a new type of cargo distribution system and then went on to found Federal Express. Federal Express officially began operations in 1973 and set the standard for the express shipping industry. Just a few years later, after the airline industry deregulated, the passenger air carriers started using the same hub-and-spoke model that Federal Express, now known as FedEx, pioneered. The cargo industry often uses aircraft that have been retired from passenger service, modified for cargo carriage. In this photograph, a DC-10 sits on the cargo ramp at DIA. (Courtesy of DEN.)

Shortly after the opening of DIA, stories started to emerge about secret underground bunkers, alleged apocalyptic-themed artwork, UFOs, and a New World Order government, to name just a few. Numerous websites and television documentaries speculate about what is "really going on" at the airport in Denver. Nearly everything about the airport has been tied into the theories at one point or another, including the layout of the runways to the baggage tunnels under DIA. Even the 1978 Steven Spielberg movie *Close Encounters of the Third Kind* has been connected to the airport. In the movie, aliens broadcast the latitude and longitude of the alien landing site, which is supposed to be Devil's Tower in Wyoming. Some conspiracy theorists believe the coordinates (40.36° N/104.44° W) are the actual coordinates for Denver International Airport, which would not open until 17 years after the movie premiered. The coordinates actually lead to a point 11 miles north and slightly east of DIA, but if those coordinates are put into Google Earth, it will zoom in on the airport. In 2016, the airport decided to embrace the theories and set up a Conspiracy Theories Uncovered gallery, complete with a fake alien skull on display. The skull was made by employees and planted during construction of the airport hotel and transportation center. (Both, courtesy of DEN.)

Adding to the conspiracy theories is DIA's famed blue horse, officially named *Blue Mustang.* The horse was delivered and unveiled to DIA in 2008. It's a 32-foot, 9,000-pound, electric-blue, anatomically correct fiberglass sculpture of a rearing horse situated along Peña Boulevard. However, shortly after the horse was put into place, locals nicknamed him "Blucifer" after his fire-red eyes, which glow brightly into the night sky. (Courtesy of DEN.)

Sadly, Luis Jiménez, the New Mexico sculptor of *Blue Mustang*, died in 2006 after a piece of the horse fell on top of him, pinning him to the ground. Family, friends, and the artist's staff completed the work in Jiménez's honor. (Photograph by Jeffrey Price.)

As of 2018, Colorado ranked No. 1 in sector employment per capita in aerospace jobs. Several large aerospace companies, including Lockheed, Ball, and Raytheon have operations in the Colorado area. The companies often have to fly rocket components into and out of the state, and the size of DIA enables some of the largest aircraft in the world to takeoff and land. In this photograph, an Antonov-124 is loaded with a rocket component at DIA. (Courtesy of DEN.)

Early designs for DIA called for a hotel to be located just east of the concourse A bridge, across from the Airport Office Building, and for a light rail line to connect downtown Denver to the airport. The Westin hotel opened at the south end of the terminal building in 2015, and the A-Line commuter rail line opened in 2016. Passengers can pay $9 one way to get from the airport to Denver Union Station. (Above, courtesy of Shahn Sederberg; below, photograph by Jeffrey Price.)

Six

Everything's Changed

Air Travel Then and Now

As an industry, aviation is not that old; however, aviation technology has come a long way since the first powered aircraft took to the skies. As commercial airliners developed, air travel became a luxury of the rich, with a passenger paying $138 for a round trip from Chicago to Phoenix; in 2017 dollars, that is about $1,100. Airline deregulation brought air travel to the masses, and as it moved into the 21st century, flying was as routine as rail travel was in the mid-1920s. September 11, 2001, reminded everyone that aviation is still a fragile system, as the terrorist attacks not only caused the deaths of nearly 3,000 people, but also sent the economy into a recession, and the after-effects were felt for years. However, the industry bounced back, as it always has, and today, people are traveling farther and faster than most of aviation's original pioneers could have ever imagined. Along the way, Denver as a city struggled to find its way into the new frontier. First it was ignored by the pioneers, who headed either north or south to avoid the highest peaks of the Rockies. Then the wagon trains and the railroads followed. Even the airmail routes were initially established through Cheyenne, with the belief that even an airplane could not successfully navigate over the mountains. Through it all, the people of Denver demanded that their city be a critical part of the economy and the growth of the nation. (Courtesy of DPL.)

One of the most significant changes in air travel in the past two decades was the effect of September 11, 2001, on the travel experience. DIA's three screening checkpoints were designed in a pre-9/11 world. At the time, checkpoints did not require a lot of room, the screening process only took a few minutes, and there had only been a handful of situations involving active shooters or bombs left in airports. The photograph above shows the DIA north screening checkpoint in August 2001. The image below shows DIA's checkpoint in 2017. Airport planners have had to make massive amounts of floor space available for the checkpoint operations, and now must consider the vulnerability of large numbers of people waiting in lines, which creates a target for shootings and bombings. (Both, courtesy of Jeffrey Price.)

Another significant change brought on by the terrorist attacks is that friends and family can no longer accompany passengers to the gate, nor pick them up at the gate. Above, passengers wait with loved ones to board a United Airlines flight in the mid-1970s at Stapleton International Airport. The photograph below shows the typical passenger farewell at Denver International Airport today. Whereas pre-9/11, friends and family could wave to their loved ones from the gate as the plane taxied away, now they wave goodbye when passengers pass into security. (Above, photograph by Zig Price; below, photograph by Jeffrey Price.)

Early airport Flight Information Display Screens (FIDS) were often cathode ray tube screens displaying standard flight information, as seen in the photograph above of a set of FIDS monitors at Stapleton International Airport. Modern digital FIDS screens convey large amounts of information, including messages to passengers, emergency information, and more up-to-date flight information. (Above, courtesy of DEN; below, photograph by Jeffrey Price.)

Above, a passenger is provided guidance from an information booth airport service representative at Stapleton International Airport around the mid-1980s. Below, an airport ambassador stands ready to give guidance, information, or advice to passengers in Denver International Airport. DIA was one of the first airports to start the ambassador program, which takes volunteers from the community, mostly retired, and provides vests and hats that are reflective of Colorado's frontier spirit, who are then available to help passengers throughout the day. (Above, courtesy of DEN; below, photograph by Jeffrey Price.)

The traveling public rarely sees one of the areas of an airport that is critical to its safe and secure operation: the airport operations center. Above, an airport operations representative works at the security station in the Stapleton Communications Center around the early 1990s. The communications center featured airfield maps, weather system monitors, a TV that could access any of the closed-circuit cameras throughout the airport, and radio and telephone systems. Below, the Denver International Airport communications center has increased in size tremendously. All of the same functionalities that were at Stapleton are still in DIA's center, but the number of cameras that can be viewed are in the thousands, and the police dispatch center has been incorporated. A similar room on the same floor houses the maintenance control center, combined with the Automated Guideway Transit System command center. All of the centers are open 24 hours a day and provide assistance to airport operations managers in the airfield, terminal and ground transportation, and parking areas. (Above, photograph by Jeffrey Price; below, courtesy of DEN.)

Passengers tend to think that the FAA operates airports, but with few exceptions, cities, counties, and airport authorities are the operator of most every civilian, public-use airport in the United States. The FAA provides separation of air traffic and clears pilots to take off and land, but it is the job of airport operations to look for and solve problems that could affect the safe, secure, and efficient movement of passengers, baggage, cargo, and aircraft through the airport. For many, airport operations is an entry gate to a career in airport management or other areas such as airport planning, air service development, maintenance, or emergency management. With the size of DIA, there is one senior "ops" manager on duty, with several assistant operations personnel specializing in the airfield, terminal operations, ramp control, or "landside," which includes the parking lots, taxi queues, and other public areas outside the airport. The core tools of an airside operations manager are their vehicle, a radio, and a symbol of authority, often a jacket with Airport Operations emblazoned on the back. The photograph above shows an airport operations vehicle in the late 1980s. The image below shows DIA's modern-day operations vehicles, which can be used to rapidly set up a temporary incident command post. (Above, courtesy of DEN; below, photograph by Jeffrey Price.)

As much as the airport has changed over time, so has the background and education of those who operate them. Most early airport managers were former or current pilots or worked for the airlines. Many civilian airport manager jobs were filled with pilots retiring from the military who could no longer fly, or those who wanted to be a pilot but could not meet the medical requirements. Today, airport operators and managers are far better educated and more of them are choosing a career in managing airports. There is an entire career field and knowledge base, baccalaureate and advanced degrees, and certifications and accreditations in the airport management industry. Above, in 1997, an assistant airport operations manager scans Denver's airfield. Below, in 2017, operations manager Heather Bowman watches a United Express regional jet taxi by. (Both, photographs by Jeffrey Price.)

Airline differential pricing models and passenger categories based on airfares, frequent flyer miles, and other factors have changed another aspect of air travel. Above, passengers at Stapleton International Airport casually wait for their Braniff flight to board in the 1970s. Below, in 2018, passengers line up in their assigned boarding group to board a United Airlines flight. Nearly all airlines use some type of line-boarding system, but many gate areas were not designed for the long lines. The phenomenon comes as a result of airline checked-bag fees and the race for overhead bag space. (Above, courtesy of DEN; below, photograph by Jeffrey Price.)

Above is the highly complex automated baggage system originally designed and constructed at Denver International Airport. The system has been completely deconstructed and sold off. At left is the alternate baggage system, which is the standard tug-and-cart distribution system. (Both, courtesy of DEN.)

Pictured above is a United Airlines DC-10 departing Stapleton International Airport in the 1960s. At right is a sampling of United's fleet looking from the concourse B ramp control tower. Modern aircraft fly faster and farther, taking advantage of better engine and aerodynamic fuel efficiencies, and use engines that are quieter and produce less harmful emissions. (Both, courtesy of DEN.)

Above is the great hall of Stapleton International Airport. While Stapleton was adorned with some artwork, Denver International Airport has become a virtual second Denver art gallery with permanent and temporary displays. The airport has its own special events section that plans movie nights, an ice rink in the winter, and numerous other events to bring people who are not flying out to the airport. This helps make DIA a destination for entertainment not just for flight, which increases airport revenue and keeps costs down. At left, 140 giant paper airplanes are suspended from the ceiling, hanging over the escalators that bring passengers up from the trains into the main terminal. Created by sculptor Patty Ortiz, they point arriving passengers to the main terminal. (Both, courtesy of DEN.)

The Jeppesen Terminal was originally designed with the thought that when expansion was necessary, the entire terminal building could be duplicated (on the south side) and attached to the existing terminal. However, with the September 11 terrorist attacks and other changing dynamics in the aviation industry, the spot where DIA could expand its terminal is now the location of the Westin Hotel and the commuter rail station. The image above shows the original configuration, and below is the facility in 2018. The dip in the top of the hotel is both for aesthetics, as it can represent a set of wings, and also so the FAA control tower personnel can see over the terminal building to the south cargo ramp. (Above, courtesy of DEN; below, photograph by Jeffrey Price.)

This mid-1980s photograph shows Stapleton International Airport in its heyday. A variety of airlines are seen on the ramp including Delta, Continental, TWA, and United. Visible in this picture is the air-traffic control tower and concourse B, immediately left of the tower. In the foreground is concourse D, with concourse C in the middle. The general aviation ramp can be seen at the very top, on the other side of the east-west runway complex. (Courtesy of DEN.)

Today, a large mixed-use residential community sits on the site of the former Stapleton airport. The tower was the only structure left standing and is the site of a new restaurant. A long park now winds through the subdivisions where the former east-west runway complex used to be. (Photograph by Austin Price.)

Denver mayor Federico Peña said, "I hope it will be said of our effort, when history sits in judgment, that we reached out far beyond our borders and helped shape the world's aviation future. That here at the foot of the Rockies, we held fast to our vision and achieved the fullest potential of our city and its people." (Photograph by Jeffrey Price.)

Bibliography

Dempsey, Paul Stephen, Andrew R. Goetz, and Joseph S. Szyliowicz. *Denver International Airport: Lessons Learned*. New York, NY: McGraw-Hill, 1997.

Garvey, William, and David Fisher. *The Age of Flight: A History of America's Pioneering Airline*. Greensboro, NC: Pace Communications, 2002.

Miller, Jeff. *Stapleton International Airport: "The First Fifty Years."* Boulder, CO: Pruett Publishing Co., 1983.

Murray, Laura K. *The Story of Southwest Airlines*. Mankato, MN: Creative Education, 2016.

Serling, Robert J. *Maverick: The Story of Robert Six and Continental Airlines: Robert J. Serling*. Garden City, NY: Doubleday, 1974.

Sommers, Jessica. *Fentress Bradburn Architects: Gateway to the West: Designing the Passenger Terminal Complex at Denver International Airport*. Mulgrave, Australia: Images Publishing Group, 2000.

Stearns, Gregory R. *Frontier Airlines: A History of the Former Frontier Airlines, 1950–1986*. Atglen, PA: Schiffer Military History, 2012.